Sex Explicit Short Stories Box Set:

Naughty Fantasies, Taboo Sex Stories, BDSM, Cuckold, How to Talk Dirty, Domination & Submission, Gangbang

Tantric Sex

Ancient Hindu Practice to Expand Your Sexual Energy, Experience Mind-Blowing Sex and Overcome Taboo of Kama Sutra. Level up Your Sex Life and Learn Tantric Massage.

© Copyright 2019 by CHASECHECK LTD - All rights reserved.

The content contained within this book may not be reproduced, duplicated or transmitted without direct written permission from the author or the publisher.

Under no circumstances will any blame or legal responsibility be held against the publisher, or author, for any damages, reparation, or monetary loss due to the information contained within this book. Either directly or indirectly.

Legal Notice:

This book is copyright protected. This book is only for personal use. You cannot amend, distribute, sell, use, quote or paraphrase any part, or the content within this book, without the consent of the author or publisher.

Disclaimer Notice:

Please note the information contained within this document is for educational and entertainment purposes only. All effort has been executed to present accurate, up to date, and reliable, complete information. No warranties of any kind are declared or implied. Readers acknowledge that the author is not engaging in the rendering of legal, financial, medical or professional advice. The content within this book has been derived from various sources. Please consult a licensed professional before attempting any techniques outlined in this book.

By reading this document, the reader agrees that under no circumstances is the author responsible for any losses, direct or indirect, which are incurred as a result of the use of information contained within this document, including, but not limited to, — errors, omissions, or inaccuracies.

Table of Contents

Introduction
Chapter 1: The Philosophy of Tantric Sex
    Defining tantric sex
    Tantric sex and love
    Tantric sex is a mindset
    The slower, the better
    Taking the leap
Chapter 2: The Difference Between Sex and Tantric Sex
    Difference #1: It's not about orgasm
    Difference #2: It's a sensory experience
    Difference #3: There is no domination or control
    Difference #4: Nothing else matters
    Difference #5: Surrender at all times
Chapter 3: The Need for Tantric Sex
    Sex is meant to be enjoyable
    Traditional sex gets old… fast
    Good sex is key to a healthy life
    Making orgasms count
Chapter 4: Setting the Scene
    Talk with your partner about what they want
    Setting up the right visuals
    Taking in the sounds
    Lighting to set the mood
    Using scents to your advantage
    Things don't always happen in the bedroom
Chapter 5: Fostering Intimacy and Touching
    Fostering intimacy
    Building intimacy every day
    The role of trust in building intimacy
    The power of touch
    Using touch effectively
Chapter 6: Breathing and Relaxation
    The role of relaxation in tantra
    Calming your mind
    Syncing your breathing
    Don't forget to breathe!
Chapter 7: Using Toys

Talking it over
Toys during warm-up
Toys during intercourse
How to determine if toys are right for you
Not all toys are created equal
Getting over the mental hang up

Chapter 8: Exercises During Tantric Sex
Going solo
Solo exercise #1: Meditation
Solo exercise #2: Self-massaging
Solo exercise #3: Masturbation
Working with a partner
Team exercise #1: Foreplay
Team exercise #2: Snuggling or cuddling
Team exercise #3: Sex

Chapter 9: Positions During Tantric Sex
Going on the power play
Take things slow
The final lap
The reverse lap
Spooning
Mutual masturbation

Chapter 10: Massages During Tantric Sex
Massaging roles
Setting the stage
Using equipment
The proper technique
Happy ending?
What to watch out for

Chapter 11: What is Tantric Pleasure?
What is tantric pleasure?
All about physical pleasure
Establishing an emotional connection
Building a spiritual connection
Using tantra as a means of deepening connections

Chapter 12: The Male Orgasm
How arousal works
Getting to the big "O."
Making sense of male pleasure

Chapter 13: The Female Orgasm
    Arousal in women
    What's holding you back
    Getting to the big "O."
    The path to the big "O."

Chapter 14: Individual Ecstasy
    Helping your partner find ecstasy
    Relaxation is the key
    Being supportive and understanding
    It's a two-way street

Chapter 15: Couples Ecstasy
    Taking turns
    Reaching the big "O" together
    After the grand finale
    One final consideration

Conclusion

Introduction

Welcome to tantric sex. If this is your first time with tantra and the power it can bring to your sex life, then you don't know what you have been missing. You are in for a real treat. After reading this book, you will never go back to your old sex life ever again. This book is about the art of tantric sex and how it can be used to increase your sexual energy to the limit of your capabilities. You will find that true, tantric experience is truly mind-blowing. When you reach the heights of sexual pleasure and ecstasy, you will become a completely different person. In fact, don't be surprised if you discover a whole new way of looking at life. Now, this book is not a mere collection of sex positions and boring role plays. Those are just games. This book is meant to be your pathway to a life-altering experience that will leave you profoundly changed. It will make you and your partner achieve new levels of sexual connection, unlike you have ever felt.

Be prepared to challenge everything you have seen and heard about tantra. In these pages, you will find everything you need to know about making your sex life everything you have wanted it to be. So, if you thought you knew about tantra, prepared to be blown away… literally.

But don't worry if you haven't experienced tantra before. This book is meant to take you through a gradual process in which you will discover your own sexual energy and combine it with your partner. You'll find that the powerful connection that is created can lead to unbelievable heights of pleasure.

If you have experienced tantra in the past, then you have an idea of just how powerful it can be. However, this book will challenge your current perceptions and take you to the next level. As you go further in this book, you will uncover new levels that never knew were there.

So, the time has come to uncover the wonderful and magical side of tantric sex. The time has come to explore your sexuality and discover your partner's own desires and fantasies. Together, you can take things to the level which you have always wanted to. However, there is one word of caution: the concepts, ideas, practices, and techniques in this book build on each other gradually. This means that if you, or your partner, are new to tantra, it's best to take it easy at first. It's important to take your time as tantra is not something that you can use right out of the box. It takes some time before you can truly master it. But when you do, you, there will be no turning back. Your partner, or partners, will look to you as "the one."

Let's get started on this journey to a world you have always wanted to explore, but perhaps didn't have the chance to. So, here it is. Here's your chance to make your sex life everything you have wanted it to be.

Chapter 1: The Philosophy of Tantric Sex

Sex is an important part of our lives. Regardless of your preferences and/or orientations, sex is a vital component to making our lives full and complete. Without it, it can be quite difficult to lead a healthy and productive life. In fact, the longer you go without it, the harder it can be to function properly in life. Now, it should be noted that there is a difference between sex and tantric sex.
Regular, run of the mill sex (which we will be referring to as "traditional sex") is an act which virtually all humans go through at some point in their lives. Unfortunately for some, they go through traumatic experiences with sex. This is something that cannot be disregarded and has an important place in tantra. How so?
Well, sex is about a physical, emotional, and psychological experience that is meant to take us to heights of pleasure, intimacy, and connection. Sex is about connecting with your partner (or partners, as the case may be) in such a way that you are able to mutually satisfy each other. This mutual satisfaction can lead to a connection that brings out the best in both of you. Of course, there is a place for love and romance. But as far as this book is concerned, love and romance are a separate topic. The reason for this is that love and romance are not pre-requisites to having a magical experience with tantric sex. In fact, you can conjure up an amazing experience with someone you have barely met. This is possible if you know what you are doing.
Moreover, tantric sex differs from traditional sex in the sense that you are focusing on both yourself and your partner. This is the crux of the matter. If you are selfish and don't pay close attention to your partner's needs, then your sexual encounter won't result quite as good as you might have hoped for.
In fact, if you're plan is to get off and have a merry old time, then tantric sex may not be the most effective philosophy for you. If you're just looking for fun and creative ways to spice up your sex life, then you'll be quite surprised to find that tantric sex goes far beyond that.

When you are committed to making your own sexual experience the best it can be by making your partner's experience as good as it can be, then you know you're in the tantra ballpark. Please bear in mind that this isn't about looks, size, or stamina; this is about knowing what buttons to push and when to push them. Master that, and you will forever go down in history as one of the best.

If that seems like an outrageous claim, don't worry. Once you see what tantric sex can do, especially to someone who hasn't really experienced it before, you'll frame this page up on your wall.

Defining tantric sex

Sadly, most so-called gurus and sexperts pass off tantric sex for a collection of funky positions that don't really anywhere. Sure, it can be fun to try out some new positions, but at the end of the day, if you don't add all of the components that make up a tantric session, then you will be coming up short.

Tantric sex can be viewed as focusing on slow intercourse. This isn't about banging away until everyone comes. In fact, orgasm is not the main focus on tantra.

Does that seem surprising?

If you are unfamiliar with tantric sex, then it surely does seem surprising.

Tantric sex is about synchronizing movements, breathing, eye contact, touching, and even orgasms… it's all about taking your partner and leading the way. As your partner follows along, you can connect with them in such a way that everything moves in concert. Each movement, thrust, breath, touch, and so on, is done with a clear intention in mind.

Of course, there is always room for a quick romp.

But that's not what tantra is about. Tantra is about finding the right place and the right time to get it on. If you are in a hurry, then tantra's not for you. You need to focus and take your time. Otherwise, you won't be able to hit the heights you expect.

Tantric sex and love

If you are planning to engage in tantric sex with a loving and committed partner, you will find that your sexual encounters will become unforgettable. Tantra becomes easier when you have a history with your partner in such a way that you are both comfortable with each other and have a high degree of trust. However, this doesn't mean that you have to be in love with them.

As a matter of fact, it is quite common to find tantra practitioners who hook up just because they know they are going to be in for a real treat. When two experienced practitioners get together, fireworks light up. As such, you don't need to be in love with your partner, though it certainly helps if you are.

It should also be said that tantric sex isn't really a one-night stand type of thing. If you believe that you can hook up with someone on a random night and have a mind-blowing tantra session, then you might be disappointed.

Ideally, tantra works with someone you know, someone you trust and with whom you can build a connection. That is something which you can't really do with someone you meet at a club or a bar. Often, it takes some time to get to know someone before you can really go through the roof in a tantra session.

Tantric sex is a mindset

When you really get into tantric sex, you'll find that it's mostly a question of mindset. When your head is not in the game, tantra doesn't work. You see, tantra is about making your energy flow. When this energy flows, it's like an electric charge that pulsates through your body. As this charge courses through your entire being, your partner will pick up on that. As your partner's energy flows as well, then a circuit is complete. This circuit enables the energy to flow through both of you.

That is why tantra isn't about orgasm; it's about prolonging the experience as much as possible. But that doesn't mean that you have to go for hours. In fact, those who master tantra are quite efficient at achieving orgasm (we'll be defining that in a bit).

That being said, tantric sex isn't about spending hours in bed. It can be something as short as 10 or 15 minutes. But even if it's just 15 minutes, if your mind is really into it, you can achieve pleasure that will literally blow you away.

Please keep in mind that focus is key. You can't expect to have a full tantric experience while you are concerned about this thing or that thing. Most experienced tantra practitioners find that disconnecting while in a tantra session is a means of release. So, turn off your phone and forget about emails. When you are ready for a tantric session, the world around you goes away. All you need to focus on is you and your partner.

In a manner of speaking, tantra is like mindfulness. Mindfulness is about focusing on the "here" and the "now." This is why you will hear tantra experts say that tantra is like meditating. And when you truly think about, that's what it is. Tantric sex is like meditating on your sexual energy.

The slower, the better

One of the worst things modern culture has taught people is that fast and hard are the "hottest" ways to have sex. You often see that in movies, TV shows, and books. Perhaps the worst of all is pornography. Most porn films feature fast and aggressive movements that don't really foster any kind of connection. After all, porn is just acting.

This is the main reason why porn is so damaging to those who believe that real sex is like porn films. When you break it down, going as hard as you can, while exciting to a certain degree, does not foster the connection and intimacy that is needed to achieve real tantric ecstasy.

Consequently, the phrase, "the slower, the better" ought to become your new mantra. If you get it in your head that taking your time is the way to go, then you will find that opening the door to tantra is quite easy.

Of course, going slow can be hard for some, especially men. For guys, it can be hard to go slow, and controlling arousal and orgasm can be a real challenge. This is why tantra is not something you can just read through and put it to use. Tantra is the type of practice that needs time and dedication.

But there is some good news. The practices we will outline throughout this book will help those who have trouble controlling their arousal find the means of settling down and allowing their energies to really flow. This is why the mantra, "the slower, the better" will make all the difference in the world.

Taking the leap

Now that we have defined what tantric sex is all about, you are ready to take the leap into the world of pleasure. So, to kick things off, make a concerted effort to put your current way of looking at sex behind you. Now, make a conscious decision to embrace a new way of looking at sex. This new way is based on being open-minded. When you are truly open-minded, you are open to the new experiences you are about to encounter.

Please don't think we're talking about bondage or that sort of thing (well, if you're into it…) We're talking about being open-minded in such a way that you are focused on experiencing everything that sex has to offer you, everything from a wonderful physical experience to a deep, emotional connection. With that mindset, you can't go wrong.

If you are in a committed relationship, then please take the time to talk about this with your partner. Talk about what you expect from your sex life. By talking about it, you can both be on the same page. This will allow your tantric sessions to be focused on what fulfills you.

For instance, some couples value touching and kissing a lot more than penetration. Other couples place a higher emphasis on rhythmic movements as if they were dancing. Other couples value the sensory perception of their encounters above everything else. A good example of sensory perception can be scents or sounds that are arousing or soothing.

As you can see, there really is no "standard" way of enjoying tantra. There isn't some formula that you need to follow. Sure, there is a path you must go down, but at the end of the day, this path leads to different outcomes. In fact, don't be surprised to find that practicing tantra with different partners leads to completely different results. Naturally, everyone is different, so it's logical to assume experiences will be different, too.

So, here is your first exercise: the next time you have intercourse with your partner, try to set the stage so that you have no interruptions or distractions. This means no phones, no gadgets, no nothing. If you must get away somewhere, then do it. It could even be just booking a hotel room in your city. The point is to devote your entire time and attention to your partner, even if it's just a couple of hours. The secret here is to give your undivided attention to what you want and what you want to give your partner. That alone is enough to make your next sexual encounter a great one. So, please get into the habit of blocking out the world around you and focusing your energies and attention on your partner and nothing else. It's totally worth it!

Chapter 2: The Difference Between Sex and Tantric Sex

At the beginning of our sex lives, we don't really know what to do or what to expect. Even when your parents give you "the talk," you really don't know what's happening until you actually do it. Then, depending on the amount of sex education you get, you learn more and more about sexuality and how it actually works.

However, most people don't really take the time to learn as much as they can about sex. It's funny that we should act in this manner, especially since sex is such a significant part of human life. In fact, most of what we learn is generally on the fly. For example, you hook up with someone who's older and more experienced, they show you what to do, and that's that.

For some guys and gals, teaching a virgin about sex is a thrill they relish. Then, there are some who are caring and strive the show a younger partner how to really enjoy. Sadly, these people and experiences are hard to come by.

That is why your interest in this book is a testament to your desire to learn about the best ways in which you can unleash your sexual potential. Through the art of tantric sex, you can unlock all of the repressed energy within you.

Yes, that's right, repressed energy.

Even if you have intercourse ten times a day, the energy is stuck there within you. Your sexual energy is never released unless you give it the time it needs to fully unfold and envelope you. When you are open to such experiences, you allow your core to absorb every minute detail of intercourse.

In this chapter, we are going to explore five important differences between traditional sex and tantric sex. These differences will enable you to have a crystal-clear understanding of what tantric sex and what it can do to improve your sexual life exponentially.

So, let's get right into it.

Difference #1: It's not about orgasm

When most folks think about sex, they see orgasm as the ultimate goal. This is particularly true for most men. Most guys tend to believe sex begins with arousal and ends with orgasm. In between, there is intercourse. However, intercourse is just a means to an end, so to speak.

This mentality is detrimental to a healthy and fulfilling sex life as sex, itself, is much more than the mere act of intercourse. In a manner of speaking, it's like reducing a meal to just dessert. So, instead of enjoying every bit of food in your meal, you simply rush through the first course just to get to dessert. Once dessert is served, you wolf it down and be done with it.

When you look at sex in this manner, you won't ever truly enjoy everything it has to offer you. In fact, it even seems transactional to a certain degree. That is why sex is much more than just reaching orgasm. It's about the entire experience surrounding the encounter.

For a lot of women, reaching orgasm can be a challenging endeavor. Often, this is due to the lack of synchronicity with their partner. There are times when it seems that there is no communication whatsoever. When this happens, one partner gets off, and the other… may not.

That is why the entire scene that surrounds tantra begins well before actual coitus. It begins with both partners fostering intimacy. It begins with being in touch with each other's needs and desires. From there, the overall experience of the encounter makes sex much more enjoyable. At that point, orgasm is a natural consequence. For women, this can lead to multiple orgasms. And, believe it or not, it can also lead to multiple orgasms for men (yes, that's right!)

Difference #2: It's a sensory experience

Sex goes beyond the mere act of intercourse, be it through penetration, touching, or oral. It involves all of the senses in such a manner that everything works in sync. When all senses are involved in a single encounter, the sensory experience is much broader.

This is what leads to the mind-blowing experience.

When you are committed to a full sensory experience, you begin sex with visuals such as dressing up (whatever you fancy is perfectly fine), sounds such as music or any other auditory stimulus, smell such as your favorite scents, touch such as massaging, and of course, taste (food and drink can also be part of the experience).

To put this into perspective, think of all the mating rituals that humans go through prior to hitting the sack. For example, dance is a powerful mating ritual. The most sensual dances mimic sexual movements in such a manner that they foster intimacy among the couple. When a couple is able to hit it off on the dance floor, they can be confident they can hit it off in bed. While this doesn't necessarily constitute a guarantee, it's a heck of a place to start.

Another powerful mating ritual is food. This is the reason why most dates (especially first dates) involve food in one way or another. Also, drink plays a vital role in mating rituals. Just look at films and TV shows. Most dates begin with dinner and drink, and then end up in the sack. The sensory perception that is built with food and drink carries over into coitus.

So, if you are keen on really getting a full, tantric experience, don't skimp on the entire event leading up to sex. While it is not necessary for you to put together an elaborate evening, it is certainly helpful if you set the stage in this manner. This can be especially helpful while you learn the ways of tantric sex. Eventually, you won't need such an elaborate setup.

Difference #3: There is no domination or control

One of the most interesting dynamics of traditional sex is the need for domination and/or control. Sure, most couples have one partner who leads, and the other tends to follow along. But in the world of tantra, this isn't about having one partner dominate the other such as in the world of BDSM. The fact of the matter is that tantra practitioners don't seek power, domination, or control. What they seek is to please their partner, and as a result, themselves.

Now, that happens if you are naturally dominant? Does that mean that there is no place for you in the world of tantra? That's hardly the case!

In fact, dominant individuals take great pleasure in guiding their partner through the road that leads to pleasure and ecstasy. This is the ultimate rush that a dominant individual can derive from tantra.

Think about that…

What could be better than blowing your partner's mind? Imagine how incredibly satisfying it can be to give your partner the best sex of their lives… this is a feeling you can't get from "dominating" your partner.

You see, in traditional dom-sub relationships, the dom derives pleasure from the power rush that comes from having their sub at their mercy. This is a one-way relationship in which the sub doesn't always derive pleasure from their position. In fact, there are many cases that subs go along with the game simply because they want to feel "loved" in some way. As such, subs comply with their dom's bidding with the hope of gaining the dom's favor.

While this type of dynamic works perfectly well for some couples, it's not the type of relationship that is built for mutual pleasure and fulfillment. This is one of the reasons why dom-sub relationships tend to run their course; that is, they aren't meant to be long-term relationships.

With tantric sex, the focus is on mutual satisfaction and fulfillment. This implies that all parties have the chance to get what they want out of the relationship. Now, it should be noted that "relationship" doesn't mean a romantic partnership. If anything, a tantric relationship can be strictly sex with no strings attached. But the relationship and the dynamic that evolves from the practice of tantra can lead to a relationship that is far more fulfilling than your run-of-the-mill romantic partnership.

Difference #4: Nothing else matters

This is one of the biggest mistakes that couples make: they let other things get in the way during their encounters. Please bear in mind that tantric sex is about the here and the now. So, when you are getting it on, nothing else matters.

This concept doesn't apply just to phones and email. It also applies to anything else that might be creeping up in your mind. For example, if you are concerned about your physical appearance, say, you're concerned about being overweight, then you will find that you won't be able to get as much out of your encounters as you'd like. Based on this concept, you really, truly, need to let go.

So what if you're not physically perfect?

So what if you're not the biggest?

So what if you're not the most attractive?

If you are attractive and desirable to someone who is willing to engage in tantric sex with you, then it's just a matter of going with it. In the end, you'll enjoy the relationship far more simply because you are able to let go of your hang-ups.

The fact of the matter is that we get in our own way. Most of the time, there is genuine attraction and chemistry. But when you don't give yourself a chance to really enjoy intercourse, then you find your mind more concerned about a million other things. Needless to say, this isn't the most exciting mindset.

The overwhelming majority of tantra practitioners would much rather get with someone who shares their same mindset rather than someone who's merely good-looking. This means that tantric sex is much more than just looking good; it's about being able to translate your passion and desire into a tangible force that can open up the floodgates to amazing experiences of pleasure and ecstasy.

Difference #5: Surrender at all times

By "surrender," we're not talking about some kind of domination thing. We're talking about letting yourself go and giving yourself to your partner. This is the core tenet of tantric sex. You must be willing to give all of yourself, even for a brief moment, before you are truly able to channel your energy into the powerful force that tantric sex can unleash. If you are holding back, then you won't be able to fully harness your sexual energy.

If you are a more submissive person by nature, this might be easier to achieve. By nature, you don't need to be in control. So, it's far easier to simply go with it. But for naturally dominant individuals, surrendering may represent a monumental challenge.

Surrender happens at various levels. Firstly, anyone who engages in sexual intercourse (unless it is against their will) surrenders physically. Often, folks think this is the last thing you surrender. That could not be farther from the truth!

Surrendering your body in the act of passion is one of the easiest things you can do. It's surrendering everything else that becomes the hardest part.

As such, the next level, the emotional level, is paramount to tantric sex. Again, we are not talking about "love" here. Love has nothing to do with tantric sex. While it certainly helps to love your partner (it certainly facilitates the process), what you really need is to be emotionally invested in what you are doing. This implies that you need to be ready to give this person all of the care and attention they need during your encounter.

This is what fosters intimacy.

Then, the third level becomes a deep, spiritual level. When you are able to achieve this level, you are able to really hit it out of the park. Your connection is so profound that mind-blowing sex becomes a regular occurrence. Again, love is not a pre-requisite. But a deep understanding of each other's wants and needs is.

So, take it upon yourself to be ready to give all of yourself to your partner, even if it is for the brief moment you are together.

Chapter 3: The Need for Tantric Sex

Throughout this book, we have talked about how important sex is in the life of humans. After all, if sex wasn't important, then there wouldn't be so much attention paid to it. It would go practically unnoticed. If anything, it would serve for reproductive purposes, and that would be the end of it.

The fact that sex is so important in our lives forces us to make sex as enjoyable as possible. That's where tantra really shines. Tantra is all about situating sex in its rightful place. By giving sex the importance it deserves, you can lead a much more satisfying and fulfilling life.

In this chapter, we are going to be taking a closer look at the need for tantric sex. Now, we're not just talking about sex in general; we're talking about tantric sex. And yes, there is a clear need for it. There is a clear need for having the best possible sexual experience of your life. If you believe that tantric sex is just about massages and playing soft music, then do read on.

Sex is meant to be enjoyable

In popular culture, sex is objectified to a degree in which it is seen as a transactional occurrence. For instance, sex is used as a currency in order to obtain benefits from people. In addition, sex is reduced to a mere physical act in which one, or hopefully both, of the parties involved, get a physical rush out of it. If you are more adventurous, group sessions (or sex with multiple partners) is seen as some type of thrill that doesn't really lead anywhere. This is where people end up feeling shallow and empty. Sure, they may be sleeping with very attractive people, but at the end of the day, they don't get as much fulfillment out of it as they would expect. In fact, this is where you see extremely attractive people debase themselves simply because they don't enjoy intercourse.

Then, you have committed and/or monogamous relationships. There are folks who view sex as a chore in such relationships. So, sex isn't about having a great time with their partner. Rather, sex is viewed as a necessary evil in the relationship. Under these circumstances, you can't expect sex to be fulfilling. At best, it

would be able to provide physical release. But the reality is that sex under those terms would only prove to be a monotonous event.
So, what can be done about it?
If you find yourself not enjoying your current sex life, then you really need to ask yourself: what do I want to get out of my sex life?
This question will lead you down a path in which you must explore what you really want to get out it. If you view sex as a currency that will get you everything you want, then tantric sex might not be right for you. However, if you view sex as something pleasurable that you would love to share with your partner (whoever that might be), then tantric sex is a must in your life.
Additionally, a healthy sex life is part of a well-rounded lifestyle. When you have a satisfying sex life, you can be sure that this will rub off on other areas of your life as well. So, there is no reason why you shouldn't strive to incorporate tantric sex into your life right away.

Traditional sex gets old… fast

Traditional sex is fun and exciting whenever you have a new partner in your life. Even the same old positions and routines become hot and steamy when you are in lust for someone. During this phase, a quick romp is enough to get your blood boiling. However, if there is no substance to your encounters, that passion can quickly fizzle out, leaving you with mundane encounters. This is why many relationships don't survive for too long.
Of course, it's true that relationships aren't solely about sex. There are other components surrounding sex which make relationships more or less enjoyable. For instance, if you and your partner share the same pursuits, then you can be sure that your relationship outside the bedroom will be fun, too. But if things aren't working as well as they could in the bedroom, then there will always be something missing.
When you look at traditional sex for what it is, physical enjoyment and attraction are the only things that can keep you

coming back for more. When attraction wears off, then there had better be something else to your relationship.

This is where tantric sex makes all the difference.

When you engage in tantra, you are moving beyond physical attraction. You are moving into a realm of emotional and even spiritual enjoyment. While you could theoretically achieve this with anyone you meet, the truth is that it doesn't happen with just anyone. It takes two people (or perhaps more…) who are willing to surrender to each other during the time they are together. Please keep this in mind at all times!

Surrendering yourself to your partner will allow you to open the floodgates of your sexual energy. Sure, there is heightened physical pleasure that comes from tantric encounters. But the fact is that the physical response is expanded by the non-physical components that are involved. In the end, the physical enjoyment you are able to get out of a tantric session will leave you feeling full. It's kind of like taking your time to savor your favorite food. In the end, you have not only enjoyed your meal but also satisfied your hunger. Ultimately, this leaves you with an amazing feeling.

Good sex is key to a healthy life

Multiple studies have shown the importance that sex has in our day to day lives. For example, sex can boost mood and improve cognitive performance. This is due to the release of chemicals by the brain after a satisfying sexual encounter.

Those studies are based on traditional sex, that is, people who engage in a "regular" sexual relationship. Now, if traditional sex can do that, imagine what tantric sex can do for you. In essence, what tantric sex does is help you circulate your sexual energy. When this occurs, it's like a wave of electricity that begins to power various aspects of your mind and body.

When you don't have sex, or you simply "get off," you don't allow your sexual energy to circulate through your body. This is why tantra calls for you to take your time. The more you rush a sexual encounter, the less chance you give your energy to flow. According to ancient beliefs, sexual energy is located at the base of the spine. From there, it moves up your spine and circulates throughout your body. And while this is an automatic process, it doesn't happen automatically.

Wait a minute…

You see, when you don't take the time to release your energy, you exert physical energy through the mechanical act of coitus, but you don't give your sexual energy the chance to get moving and flow upward. As such, the mere act of reaching orgasm doesn't necessarily imply that your sexual energy is flowing to the maximum of its capabilities.

Here's how this works:

For men, sexual pleasure is equated with ejaculation. If a man ejaculates, this implies orgasm, and all is good. However, this belief is hardly ironclad. Any guy will tell you that ejaculation does not necessarily mean orgasm. While it may feel good, it doesn't necessarily mean that a man has reached the climax of sexual pleasure.

The reason for this is that an orgasm is a chemical process that goes on in the brain. When a person reaches sexual climax, the brain floods the body with pleasure-causing chemicals. When these chemicals are released, they flow through the bloodstream and feed all of the organs and body systems. In fact, orgasm causes the penis to get harder and not softer.

Think about that for a moment…

For a man to reach orgasm, he needs to focus more on the action that is happening, on his partner's pleasure and, of course, his own. This means that he cannot be focused on how good it feels and that he can't finish too soon.

This is where he needs to let go!

He needs to forget that he is feeling pleasure and focus on the here and now. That can open the door to the chemical reactions that are produced as a result of pure sexual pleasure. In the end, a man who can master this mindset may find himself having multiple orgasms well before ejaculating once.

As for women, orgasm is a mix of emotions, physical sensations, and a sense of security. When you combine all of these elements, it's possible to reach unbelievable heights of sexual pleasure. However, women can be betrayed by their emotions. For example, if a woman feels uncomfortable about anything surrounding the encounter (such as feeling guilty about it), reaching orgasm can be quite difficult. By the same token, if she feels insecure about her physical appearance, this can also lead her to have difficulty reaching orgasm.

Again, this is why tantra is about the here and the now. When a woman is able to focus on the "task at hand," so to speak, she can let herself go. This is an emotional response in which she isn't focused on what is happening in the world around her; she is only focused on what's happening between her and her partner. That's all that matters.

Making orgasms count

One of the most common misconceptions about tantric sex is that orgasms keep coming and coming. While that may be true for some people, the fact is that it doesn't quite work that way. For many couples, having one orgasm is more than enough to make the session memorable. This is why we say you should "make orgasms count." When you really make orgasms count, the overall sensation that comes with them is incredible.

Now, it may seem paradoxical, but if you aim to reach orgasm, then it will be harder for you to get there. So, your aim in a tantric session is not to reach orgasm. Your aim should be to just enjoy it. The orgasm will come when it comes.

Do you see the difference?

When your pursuit of a sexual encounter is orgasm, you will find that it's nearly impossible to get it. It's like when you're unemployed and in need of a job. If you get desperate, you will project that in job interviews. Plus, each day that passes without a job seems like an eternity. After just a few days of job hunting, you are so stressed out and anxious that you might even get sick. The same goes for orgasms.

If you are fixated on reaching orgasm, you'll find it nearly impossible to focus on what you are actually doing. You won't be able to focus on enjoying your partner. If anything, it'll feel good up to a certain point, but nothing else.

On the flip side, if you choose to enjoy coitus for what it is, you'll find it's a lot easier to relax and let your energy flow.

When you are able to do this, reaching orgasm comes naturally. As a man, you're not worried about finished too fast. That's why you're going slow. In the case of a woman, you're not concerned that it takes you forever to reach orgasm. All you're concerned about is enjoy each passing moment with your partner.

This is the core essence of tantric sex. All of the components that make up tantric sessions are building blocks to a wonderful experience. Consequently, everything you do, from dancing to massages, is a precursor to the big "O." That way, when the big "O" does arrive, you'll be ready to literally burst at the seams. So, make every orgasm count by letting yourself go and surrendering to your partner.

Chapter 4: Setting the Scene

In tantric sex, setting the scene just right is as important as anything you do with your partner. Often, setting the scene is about setting up a comfortable atmosphere in which both of you can just be yourselves.

This is the main point here.

The right stage can make your tantric sessions that much more enjoyable. The proper atmosphere can turbocharge your senses, thereby making the overall experience memorable. In fact, having the right atmosphere alone is enough to take traditional sex into tantric territory.

But first, let's talk about what we don't mean by "setting the scene."

If you are picturing an elaborate situation in which your bedroom is flooded by candles and rose petals, then you might be taking things a bit too far. Sure, if that's the type of thing you are into, then so be it. However, you don't have to remodel your bedroom to set the right scene. If anything, you'll find that trying to hard to set the right stage will end up killing the mood altogether.

Here is a quick example:

Let's say that you want to surprise your partner with a truly special evening. So, you go pull all the stops to make your bedroom look like a scene out of a movie. You have soft music playing in the background, champagne on ice, and even some visual stimulus on the television. While this scene may seem perfect, it could backfire as it creates pressure on your partner to deliver. After all, how would you feel if your partner surprised you in this way? You'd feel pressured to make it worth their while. Of course, we're not talking about a transactional relationship, here. But, you would still feel pressured not to disappoint your partner.

Based on this example, it's plain to see that taking things too far can create unnecessary pressure on your partner. The higher you set your expectations, the harder it will be for you to enjoy yourselves.

So, let's take a look at what you can do to set the scene just right.

Talk with your partner about what they want

First and foremost, talk with your partner about what you both want in the perfect setting. It could be that you both have very simple tastes. Perhaps the décor isn't as important as privacy. Moreover, you and your partner may value quiet and darkness more than a fancy setup.
Most couples who engage in tantric sex often set their ambiance to that of peace, quiet, and privacy. The main idea here is that whatever happens in the bedroom stays in the bedroom. The last thing tantra practitioners want to worry about is the neighbors overhearing them. If they have kids, they don't want to worry about what their kids are doing while they are getting it on.
As you can see, for most folks, setting the right scene isn't so much about the visuals of a room that looks right out of a magazine. For them, it's the peace and quiet that makes all the difference. This is why it is vital that you and your partner communicate your preferences to one another.

Setting up the right visuals

Visual stimulation is essential to fulfilling tantric sex. By "visuals," we mean everything that your eyes can possibly take in. This can range from the décor and ambiance to the actual physical appearance of you and your partner.
Regarding physical appearance, anything goes!
For instance, wearing sexy lingerie, costumes, or just wearing a birthday suit can provide you with the visual stimulation you seek. Some couples enjoy dressing up with a theme in mind. Others enjoy role plays. Some prefer watching racy films to set the mood. The fact of the matter is that anything goes so long as you are both on board.
This is important to keep in mind, especially because anything that makes you or your partner uncomfortable can become a mood killer. This is the last thing you want to see happen. As such, setting any and all visuals, as long as you are both comfortable, will go a long way toward making your tantric session memorable and enjoyable.

Taking in the sounds

This is a tricky one. The traditional playbook (such as what you generally see in films) calls for soft music or smooth jazz playing in the background. However, some folks find music, or any other sound, for that matter, to be distracting. So, this doesn't mean that they don't enjoy it; it's just that background sounds may lead them to become distracted from the actual encounter itself.

To put this into perspective, imagine this situation:

Suppose you are studying for a big exam. This is an important mid-term that you need to focus all of your mental energies on. So, do you study in silence or have music blasting in the background?

Your answer to this question should give you a clear indication of how you would react to music (or any other sound) during our tantric session. In fact, it could be that you enjoy having smooth jazz playing in the background. But your partner may not. So, this is where you need to strike a balance.

One common practice is to play music while things are heating up. This could be during a massage, kissing, touching, or just cuddling. But when it comes down to intercourse, the music is off. While this doesn't mean that you are going to be in absolute silence, it does mean that there aren't any other sounds that could potentially distract you from what's going on at the moment.

In fact, turning the music off is quite useful when you are syncing your breathing. You see, when there are other noises around, it can be hard to hear your breathing. As such, you might have a hard time syncing up. But when you don't have any distracting sounds around you, it's far easier to sync your breathing. This is especially true if you close your eyes and let your other senses take over.

One other thing about sounds: don't feel compelled to make a huge ruckus during sex. One very persistent misconception is that yelling your head off is a sign of enjoyment. While that might be true for some, there are plenty of folks (women, especially) who have a mind-blowing orgasm without feeling the need to scream their head off. So, if you, or your partner, aren't the screaming type, then that's perfectly fine. Everyone is different, and it's something we need to embrace.

Lighting to set the mood

This is another one of those tricky areas. Lighting can really set the mood for you and your partner, or it can throw a monkey wrench into your session.

The rule of thumb here is that there is no rule of thumb.

Some couples feel perfectly comfortable in a well-lit area, while others prefer darkness. Again, this is all about what makes you feel comfortable. As such, it's a question of being on the same page.

In this regard, some folks like to "see what they are doing." So, a well-lit area for them works perfectly fine. They don't mind having the lights or getting it on during the daytime. For other couples, they prefer the anonymity of darkness. Thus, you'll see them drawing blackout curtains during the daytime while perhaps leaving their environment pitch black at night.

As a matter of fact, you'll find that experience tantra practitioners prefer the dark as it cancels the visuals out and forces them to feel and hear everything they are doing. For some, it's hard to concentrate when there is a large amount of visual stimulation around them. For others who are a bit more self-conscious about their physical appearance, darkness gives them the opportunity to forget about the imperfections they perceive in their body.

Once again, this is a call that you ought to make as a couple. That way, you can both feel comfortable. In the end, it's one less thing to worry about.

Using scents to your advantage

Scents are paramount in tantra. The right scents can give you the chance to focus on a different kind of sensory perception. Scents are very useful when it comes to triggering positive emotions. This is why scents are practically a cliché during massages. Everything from scented candles to essential oils is highly recommended.

When selecting scents, it's important to choose ones that trigger positive emotions. For instance, your partner is nuts for chocolate ice cream. So, using chocolate-scented oils can work wonders during a massage. In other cases, essential oils such as lavender can provide you with the olfactory stimulation you seek, that is, entering a state of relaxation.

Now, here's one naughty trick you can use to get things started in a very discreet way. Pick a scent that you both find pleasing. It could be a perfume, cologne, essential oil, scented candle, even some kind of food. Then, set a rule that this scent is only used during sexual encounters. This is a type of code that indicates that you are ready to go over the moon.

Here's the trick: use the scent well before you actually get it on. This will signal your partner what you intend to do. Even if you are nowhere near the bedroom (or your chosen place), the scent is enough to begin triggering the emotions that you associate with intercourse. By the time you actually get "down to business," your mind and body will already be in a state of readiness. In a manner of speaking, you have gotten a head start on your pleasure.

Things don't always happen in the bedroom

If you believe that an amazing tantric session only takes place in your bedroom, then you might be surprised to find that tantric sex can happen anywhere! Yes, practically any place is good for a tantric session.

To choose a place for your sessions, it must meet your criteria. Otherwise, it wouldn't work at all. Now, when we say "criteria," it's a question of meeting your requirements in terms of lighting, mood, privacy, and so on.

This means that if your garage fits the bill, then your garage would be the place to be.

It's also important to keep in mind that lifestyles are quite varied. Some couples have very busy lifestyles and so on. That's why they seek to get away from it all to be together. So, some couples find hotel rooms or go on a trip somewhere to really get it on. Ultimately, the actual location of where you do it doesn't really matter so long as it's a place that works for you. When you find this place, then you have a huge head start. Having the right place and the right atmosphere is just as important as any of the practices you can do. In fact, you could be a master practitioner of tantra, but if the mood and ambiance aren't right, you'll find that your experience just won't be the same.

At the end of the day, tantra is a combination of factors. If any factor is off, for any reason, then you might find it hard to make the most of your sessions. That's why communication is key. If you and your partner are on the same page, you will find it much easier to make the most of your time together. Even if you are naturally dominant and your partner is naturally submissive, being able to communicate what you both want is an essential part of tantra.

A healthy and rewarding sex life is all about being able to connect with your partner at a profound level. This is where tantra can lead both of you to levels you may have only dreamed about. Perhaps it might seem far away at this point. But with some careful planning and an open mind, you'll find that anything is possible in the world of tantra!

Chapter 5: Fostering Intimacy and Touching

Not everything in sex is about intercourse. Sadly, in our culture, sex is reduced to some kind of penetration, that's all there is to it. As a matter of fact, a harmful myth that persists is the belief that sex isn't really "sex" unless there is some kind of penetration. While this is certainly an important part of sex, it isn't the only part. There are so many things that can happen during an encounter. This is why you need to be aware of the various options at your disposal. Truth be told, some of the most exciting and steamy parts happen outside of traditional penetrative sex. That's why this chapter is centered on intimacy and touching. The main point is to focus on foreplay, or perhaps post-coitus activity. This is very important to keep in mind as there are so many things that can happen before and after intercourse.

Fostering intimacy

Intimacy isn't just the act of sex itself. Intimacy is an emotional connection that is felt between two individuals (or more as the case may be). You can potentially develop an intimate emotional connection with anyone without being in a committed relationship or being "in love." In fact, our lives are filled with intimate connections, such as those we cherish with family and friends. These types of intimate relationships have nothing to do with sex. It's the emotional connection that counts.

As such, it should be noted that the cornerstone of tantric sex is intimacy. Without it, achieving the truly uplifting heights of ecstasy can be hard to come by. While it is not impossible, it will take some additional effort to get there.

Fostering intimacy is not nearly as hard as you might think. The biggest step you can take with your partner(s) is to be honest about what you want, your expectations, and what you bring to the table. By being transparent in your intentions, you will find an unmatchable sense of liberation. It is so much more fulfilling to have an intimate relationship with some who you really connect with as opposed to someone with whom you have a superficial interaction.

This is the reason why mind-blowing tantric sex with a stranger is not quite that easy. It is possible if both parties are experienced in the ways of tantra. In that case, it might be quite easy for both parties to let go and surrender to the moment they find themselves in.

If you are in a committed relationship, intimacy is something that you ought to work on all the time. There are a plethora of activities that you can do to foster intimacy without even coming close to intercourse. When you make a concerted effort to foster intimacy in your day to day interactions, you will find that sex is just an extension of this usual interaction.

Building intimacy every day

Intimacy can be built every day through a clear and concerted effort to do so. For example, hugging, kissing, and meaningful touching (in a non-sexual way), is a great means of fostering intimacy.

Think about it for a minute.

If you don't even touch each other during the day, then how can you suddenly turn it on in the bedroom?

When you take the time to foster these kinds of interactions with your partner, you will find that playful touching, constant touching and kissing can easily transition into the bedroom.

What you will find is that this type of behavior simply translates into sex without much effort. In a manner of speaking, you are ready for sex all the time.

Now, what happens if you are in a long-distance relationship? In such cases, it's hard to build intimacy since you aren't physically present. This is where you need to get a bit more creative.

But before we get into it, a word of caution: if you plan to use photos and videos, please make sure that you are both on the same page about it. Unfortunately, photos and videos can fall into the wrong hands or can be misused, particularly when a relationship ends. So, it's important that all parties involved be on the same page.

That being said, the use of photos, videos, racy messages, or sexy calls over a webcam can really foster intimacy when physically separated. Please bear in mind that intimacy is more of an emotional and psychological phenomenon rather than a physical one. If anything, these types of exchanges tend to build up so much pressure that, by the time you are physically together, the fireworks are truly memorable.

In addition, building intimacy doesn't always involve racy content. Something as simple as being aware of your partner's needs on a regular basis can be enough to light a fire… and keep it burning.

The role of trust in building intimacy

When building intimacy, trust plays a key role. You have to trust your partner to some degree in order for you to be able to truly surrender yourself. This is something which can be hard when you don't really know someone.

By the same token, if there is an issue getting in between you and your partner, building trust can be quite complex. Without trust, achieving true tantric form can be more challenging. Given the fact that tantra is built on emotion and even spiritual connection, trust needs to be present at all times.

Now, it's important to note that we're not talking about trusting your partner with life and death decisions. This isn't about given them power of attorney. This is about trusting them enough to know that no harm will come to you while you are with them. This type of trust is so powerful that you know you won't have to worry about being hurt in any way. So, that leaves the door entirely open for you to relax and enjoy your encounter.

One of the biggest issues that pops up in committed relationships is infidelity. When one partner, or even both partners, are unfaithful, trust can be shot down. This drives a wedge between both partners in such a way that it may be nearly impossible to truly trust one another. As a result, this could make building your tantric experience somewhat more challenging.

If there is anything on your mind, it's best to talk about it with your partner. Get it out in the open. That way, you can clear the air and move on. That alone is enough to open the floodgates for most partners. It is incredible how unresolved issues can fester to the point where sex is no longer an enjoyable activity. In fact, sex may even become non-existent.

One other thing: it's important to discuss each other's limits. This is especially true if you are planning on engaging in some kind of BDSM activity. Trust needs to be put at the forefront of your mind. That way, you can be certain that your experience will be as pleasurable as you wish it to be. Please keep in mind that having sex with someone puts you in a vulnerable position regardless of whether you are a man or woman. So, the last thing that you want to have in mind is feeling insecure about anything that's going on during your encounter.

The power of touch

Touch is an incredibly powerful force. There is immaterial energy that is transmitted through touch. When you think about it, we can communicate so much more with a simply touching gesture than we could with words.//
This is why handshakes are so important in business communication. When you go to business seminars, trainers often tell you that a handshake says much more about your character than your resume could ever say.//
When it comes to sexual relationships, touch is a foundational element. You cannot expect to have the best sex of your life without incorporating touch in one way or another. However, not all touch is the same in the world of tantra.//
Thus far, we have talked about the kind of touch you can do outside of the bedroom. This type of touch is great at fostering intimacy while keeping you "on your toes," so to speak. It's the type of silent communication between you and your partner that says you are always ready for action, even when you really aren't.//
Now, most tantra books limit touching to sensual massages. And while we will be covering massages extensively, it's important to note that touch is so much more than that. Many times, light, sensual touching can produce unbelievable effects.

Using touch effectively

To heighten the sensation of touch, you really need to set the stage. This can be done through the atmosphere that we described earlier. In addition, hugging and cuddling can give you the opportunity to use touch effectively before you engage in actual intercourse.

Many couples enjoy genital touch, such as mutual masturbation, while cuddling and kissing. This is by no means meant to replace the entire act of coitus. However, it can be a power foreplay technique. All you need to do to make this technique effective is to relax and let go. In fact, many couples who have sex for the first time would rather spend a good deal of time touching well before engaging in intercourse.

Another important benefit of touching as part of foreplay is that it eases any anxiety prior to the main part of the show. This is important as genital stimulation allows you to become aroused at your own pace. Naturally, not everyone gets aroused in the same manner. For some, it takes longer than others. As such, touching can allow you to take all the time you need to get aroused at your own pace. That not only takes the pressure off, but it also allows you for variety.

Some tantra practitioners like to mix things up. For instance, they engage in intercourse and then separate in order to spend some time cuddling and kissing. This can be a good way of resting, particularly when you are planning to spend a good deal of time together.

Touching is incredibly useful, particularly for me. After ejaculation, there is a period in which the penis needs to recover before becoming erect again. This is a perfect time for touching. It's a way of keeping the party going without having to put additional pressure on having another erection right away.

Furthermore, touching is incredibly powerful when one partner is essentially done while the other would like to keep going. As a matter of fact, some women report that they have more powerful orgasms following oral and manual genital stimulation (particularly stimulation of the clitoris) as compared to penetrative sex. While this may seem paradoxical, it actually makes sense. You see, when you are engaged in coitus with your partner, you are more focused on pleasing them rather than yourself. But when it's you that receives all the attention, it's far easier to just let go and enjoy the moment. This is when ecstasy can be taken to powerful heights.

As for post-coitus touching, please bear in mind that true tantric intercourse is a powerful event. This implies that simply shaking hands and being on your merry way doesn't really work. There needs to be some kind of touching, kissing, or just plain cuddling to bring your encounter to a natural conclusion. While cuddling after sex may not be your thing, at least acknowledging the fact that you had an amazing time is a great way of fostering intimacy. After all, you just had a great experience with some you enjoy being with.

So, do take the time to use touching as a cool down, so to speak. This will help you bring your encounter to a natural ending while leaving you connected with your partner even if you won't see them for a while. Please keep in mind that touch makes the experience all that more powerful while ensuring that you are building an intimate bond with this amazing person.

Chapter 6: Breathing and Relaxation

When it comes to tantric sex, being in sync is absolutely paramount to an effective session. When you and your partner move as one, each movement becomes that much more enjoyable. However, being in sync isn't something that happens automatically. It's something that takes some time and effort to develop.

In this regard, breathing is of vital importance. Breathing is not only useful when it comes to regulating physical exertion, but it's also the best tool that you can use to stay on the same track. You see, tantra looks for both partners to be going down the same path together. This implies that you are focused on where you and your partner are heading as opposed to focusing on your own path toward pleasure.

In this chapter, we are going to look at the role that relaxation plays in tantra and how you can achieve this through breathing. Plus, we're going to be focusing on how breathing is the ultimate road map which can lead you and your partner down the same path toward mutual pleasure and intimate connection.

The role of relaxation in tantra

There is no question that relaxation is essential in any good tantric session. Stress, anxiety, and distractions are the most common culprits of poor sex. These factors wreak havoc on libido and desire.

Just think about that for a moment.

You are trying to get your groove on, but you can't stop thinking about a problem you had at the office. Naturally, it's an important issue that's occupying your mind. And yes, you are eager to get with your partner and have a good time. However, your head is simply not in the game.

In the case of men, this leads to added pressure, which can result in trouble getting an erection. So, on top of the anxiety and stress at the start of the session, tension mounts, even more, when the pressure is on to perform. This can be a real mojo killer.

As for women, stress and overall anxiety can lead to trouble reaching orgasm. Sure, the session might be fun and enjoyable, but things just don't feel right. So, no matter how hard she tries, she just can't seem to get there.

If you have ever been in any of these situations, you can appreciate how tough it is to not only satisfy your partner but yourself. Needless to say, this does not make for an enjoyable romp in the bedroom.

So, what can you do about it?

The first thing to consider is being honest with your partner. If you let your partner know how you feel, they can help you settle down and relax. This is crucial as your partner is there to support you. They can help you calm down and enjoy your time together. Nevertheless, that is easier said than done.

This is where breathing comes into play.

In addition to massaging, breathing is effective in relaxation. To use breathing as a relaxation technique, there isn't much that you need to do. One great exercise involves hugging and cuddling. You can sit on a sofa, lie in bed, or even stand. All you need to do is hold your partner (or be held) and simply breathe in unison. As you breathe, close your eyes and use your hands to "see" your partner's body. Don't be afraid to let your hands wander. If they should go to intimate places, then so be it! That's the whole point of the exercise.

One great way of incorporating structure into the exercise is to use rhythmic movements as if you were dancing. This could mean swaying from side to side or rubbing body parts such as the back, buttocks, genitals, breasts, or face. Each caress, each movement, each touch is intended to move in concert with each breath, that is, as you inhale and then exhale. Before you know it, you'll be moving in sync. This will eventually lead to arousal, which then leads to showtime.

Calming your mind

To say that your mind plays tricks on you is an understatement. When you are stressed out, anxious, or simply distracted, your mind gets the best of you. Consequently, you don't have the freedom to enjoy sex as much as you would like.

In fact, it's quite easy to get caught up in any number of thoughts.

For instance, you can get caught up in your physical appearance. You might end up being too overly concerned about your body to the point where you can't really enjoy what you are doing. In fact, being insecure about your body (both and men and women) can lead you to feel bad, or even guilty, about sleeping with someone.

Your mind can also have a detrimental effect on your sex life when you let it run the show. This means that you can't let your mind get the best of you during sex. For example, you can't expect to have a mind-blowing session while you are analyzing what your partner is doing, what you should do next, or why things are happening the way they are.

Even though sex does call for careful thought and consideration, once you're in the bedroom, there is no need for sex to become a mathematical equation. Yes, you need to focus on what you are doing, but this doesn't mean you should be knit-picking everything that's happening.

As a matter of fact, if things aren't going right, you can always slow things down, spend some time touching, kissing, hugging or cuddling and regroup. If you can't trust your partner enough to take a time out and regroup, then perhaps you might be better off finding someone in whom you can confide.

So, here is a great exercise which you can do to calm your mind. Now, whether you are actually having intercourse, or just getting warmed up, you can use your mind's eye to project what you want to happen. To do this, imagine that you're feeling a bright-colored light pulsating through your body. This light is coursing through every part of your being. It can start at the base of your spine and radiate onward. As you feel this energy flowing, imagine it is passing through to your partner at whatever point of contact you have. This could be through the hands, mouth, genitals, or any other point in which your bodies are in contact. Next, imagine the light enveloping the both of you. Don't pay too much attention to the pleasure you are feeling. That will be there. It's something that you can't ignore. Just imagine the light connecting both of you. This light is the energy that you are sharing during your time together. Please keep in mind that there is no need for penetration to actually take place in order for this light to pass through the both of you. All energy needs is a channel which it can run through.

Now, here is the real kicker: as this energy, in the form of light, returns to you, what you are receiving is a recycled form of energy that isn't yours anymore. It belongs to the both of you. As this energy gets stronger and stronger, the pressure builds up in such a manner that when the big "O" comes, it's explosive. However, the big "O" does just end there. It's just a means of feeding the system in a closed-loop so that the pleasure keeps building and building, thereby leading to a stronger and stronger orgasm.

Syncing your breathing

In most tantra literature, you read about the importance of syncing your breathing. It should be noted that it isn't breathing per se that leads to connection. What leads to connecting with your partner is the fact that you are both moving in unison. The role breathing plays is to enable all parties involved to progress at the same rate or at the same pace.

To sync up your breathing, especially during intercourse, here is an effective exercise:

When you are in the midst of intercourse, you might find the action getting hot and heavy. As such, it's quite common for one partner to speed up while the other is moving along at a slower rate. It's important to remember that tantric sex is about taking things slow. This means that if your partner is racing along, you can slow the pace of the game down talking to them. Tell them to breathe in and breath out with you. You can help them by modeling the way they ought to be breathing. That way, you can slow things down and sync up your breathing.

As you get into the same rhythm, the actual speed of intercourse can move from a faster and more superficial tempo to a slower and deeper one. In fact, one highly effective practice is to mix things up. You see, when the rhythm of intercourse is fast and furious, it can't possibly last very long. It's just a matter of time before one, or both, simply explode and end up unable to recover. By the time they're ready again, the moment might have already passed.

So, when you mix things up, going fast and then slowing down, you will find that it gives you the chance to better manage your pleasure (and that of your partner's) while taking the time to savor the sights and feelings. If you are looking to take in the visuals, you will have enough time to feed your sight. If you are more inclined to the sensations of it all, you will have the time to savor the moment.

Now, if things appear to be getting out of control, don't be afraid to stop and regroup. Often, all it takes is a momentary pause to regain your breathing and then resume. Please keep in mind that experienced tantra practitioners are not afraid to take a breather even when the action is hot and heavy. In doing so, you can ensure that you are making the most of the time you are spending with your partner.

Don't forget to breathe!

For a lot of folks, breathing becomes an issue at the height of pleasure simply because they forget to breathe. Yes, as silly as that may sound, there are times when you might simply forget to breathe. This occurs because your entire nervous system is fixated on the pleasure you are feeling. However, when you stop breathing, you stop supplying oxygen to your body. Now, it's not like you are going to suffocate or anything. It's just that if you are looking to really enjoy your session, it's a good idea to be cognizant of your breathing.

Breathing is a great way to keep track of yourself. You see, when things are going really well, it's easy to get so caught up that you might end up losing yourself completely. While that is not a bad thing, it might cause you to neglect your partner. This is important, especially if you are very keen on pleasing your partner.

Consider this example:

As a man, it's easy to get caught up in the moment and lose control. When you lose control, you might feel compelled to finish. While this is not the issue, there might be an issue when your partner doesn't feel that they have gotten their fair share. For instance, the other partner hasn't reached their orgasm yet. This situation exemplifies how breathing can help you stay in the moment. By focusing on breathing, both men and women can quell their mind, manage their emotions, and heighten their sensations. A simple way of using your breathing to your advantage is to simply focus on inhaling and exhaling. That's all. You don't need to count to ten, nor do you need to repeat some mantra in your mind. All you need to do is feel in the air entering your lungs and leaving your body. This alone is enough to get your body the oxygen it needs to perform up to the level you expect it to.

Chapter 7: Using Toys

One of the most common questions that surface with regard to tantric sex is the use of foreign objects, that is, "toys." Now, it should be noted that we're not talking about anything that could potentially cause harm such as artifacts used in BDSM. Also, we're not talking about any items that don't typically fall under the "sex toy" designation, such as sharp objects, machines, or even torture devices. In this discussion, we're talking about the types of things you would find in a regular sex shop such as dildos, vibrators, rings, plugs, beads, or even clamps.

Now, tantra purists will point out that textbook tantra doesn't call for the use of toys. If anything, toys can be considered as a distraction that can hinder reaching full tantric ecstasy. However, the use of toys can actually enhance pleasure particularly during a "warm-up," and especially during intercourse itself.

So, in this chapter, we are going to be discussing how you can incorporate the use of toys, should you choose to do so, under the scope of tantric sex. Moreover, we'll go over some recommended ways in which you can get the most out of the toys you bring into the bedroom.

Talking it over

Like anything in sex, the use of toys should be a mutual decision. These types of objects should not just be thrown into the mix. Sure, it might be a nice surprise, but if you haven't used toys before with a specific partner, it's always best to talk about it first.

For most women, the use of sex toys is not unheard of. In fact, you might be surprised to find most women are comfortable with the idea of using sex toys. After all, what's wrong with mixing things up a bit? The truth is that sex toys, like any other aspect of sex, are there to enhance enjoyment and pleasure.

For some men, the use of sex toys can actually be intimidating, especially if they have never used them before. This is due to the fact that the male ego may view the use of toys as a sign of dissatisfaction on the part of their partner.

This could not be farther from the truth.

A sex toy, no matter how good or pleasurable it may be, can never replace the type of interaction that comes with having sex with another person. As such, there is nothing to be worried about, or threatened by, when it comes to using sex toys.
That being said, it's important to discuss what types of toys you are both comfortable with. If you are new to the sex toy scene, perhaps you can start off with one and see how it goes. If you have had prior experience, you can talk about what you like and take it from there. By having an honest talk about what you like and what you would like to incorporate, you can ensure that your experience will be that much better.
Another important issue to talk about is boundaries. It is crucial to set your limits clearly. While you might be up for anything, there might be a certain thing you're not comfortable with, at least not yet. So, it's important to bring up these boundaries as this would avoid any potentially uncomfortable situations. The last thing you want to do is shut things down because you don't feel comfortable with anything. Please keep in mind that trust is an essential part of tantric sex.

Toys during warm-up

Prior to actual intercourse, you may choose to have a "warm-up" phase. This warmup portion of the program can be devoted to taking turns in giving and receiving pleasure.
This is where toys can really spice things up.
Consider this situation:
You are holding your partner while allowing your hands to touch all over your bodies. This touching is a great way of leading the way to arousal. Now, at this point, you might be inclined to focus on your partner's genital area. For the sake of this example, let's assume that it's a man who is stimulating a woman. The man's touch on his partner's genital area is soft and slow. The intent is to arouse his partner so that she can be receptive to intercourse. At this point, rather than jumping straight into intercourse, why not try out a toy? For instance, a vibrator can be a perfect complement to the manual stimulation in the woman's genital area. This stimulation can go as far as you want it to go.
In fact, you can even try syncing your breathing while your partner is progressively becoming more and more aroused. While

the man isn't necessarily receiving any direct stimulation, the emotional and psychological stimulation, that is, the sensory perception is a great way of boosting arousal. If you like, you can take your partner all the way to orgasm. In doing so, the woman can feel satisfied and fulfilled and… ready for more!

This example is a great way of aiding arousal. As such, toys can be used as precursors to the main event. Once in the main event, both partners can feel satisfied that they are thoroughly enjoying the situation.

Now, it should be noted that most sex toys are geared toward women. However, this doesn't mean that there aren't toys for men. It's worth taking the time to do research in order to find suitable toys based on a man's preferences. There are varying degrees of openness with regard to male sex toys, so if you're a man reading this, take some time to go through what toys are out there. If you're a woman reading this, you can peruse online catalogs with your man. That way, the experience of searching for sex toys can be a mutually bonding experience.

Toys during intercourse

The use of toys during intercourse is often debated. There are some who love the additional stimulation, while some dislike them completely. So, let's take a look at both sides of the argument.

For those who love toys during intercourse, these can provide additional stimulation. For instance, the use of clitoral vibrators during intercourse can provide another layer of arousal and stimulation. In fact, the combination of penetrative sex and clitoral stimulation can produce mind-bending orgasms. In a manner of speaking, it's like combining two foods that you love into one dish without them tasting weird.

Another facet of toys during intercourse is anal play. Some couples love using toys to stimulate the backside. This can also offer another layer of pleasure to the receiving partner. For women, anal stimulation during vaginal intercourse can produce an incredible sensation. And of course, there are men who also enjoy anal play during coitus even if they are heterosexual. Ultimately, the use of toys during intercourse is a question of finding the best way to get the most out of your experience.

On the flip side, there are those who dislike toys during intercourse altogether. The most common objection is that it becomes a distraction. For some, the use of toys during intercourse might mean fumbling in the dark for it. When looking at it from that perspective, it can certainly be seen as a distraction.

Additionally, some couples would rather not use toys during intercourse as they seek a unique experience in which it is them, and only them, who are involved in the action. While this is perfectly valid, it should also be noted that it ought to be a mutual decision. This implies that both parties should be on the same page. If one of the partners is reticent about using toys, they should at least give it a try. If they find that it's definitely not for them, then at least they gave it a try. However, it could be that once they try it, they can see just how good using toys can be.

How to determine if toys are right for you

There really is only one way to find out: try it!

If you don't try, at least once, to use toys during a tantric session, then you may never know if you are really missing out or not. It could be that you are missing out on a great experience without even knowing it. It might very well be that your hesitation about the use of toys is based on preconceptions that aren't really founded on anything.

Naturally, this argument is not intended to coerce you into trying out toys. Still, it's worth giving anything a shot at least once. In many cases, folks are reluctant to try toys out because they are afraid of being judged or seen negatively. The truth is that there is nothing wrong with the use of toys. It's just a natural part of human nature. If anything, denying yourself this opportunity can end up causing more harm than good.

Furthermore, if you commonly use toys during solo sessions (yes, both guys and gals use toys during solo sessions), then it only makes sense to carry that over into tantric sessions with your partner. As we have stated earlier, the use of toys is not about replacing your partner, or any other person for that matter, it's about enhancing the experience that you share with your partner.

Consequently, trying out toys is definitely worth a shot. If, after trying it, you feel it's not for you, then that's fair game. After all, tantric sex looks to push your boundaries. If you find yourself comfortably ensconced in your comfort zone, then you may be missing out on what could be one of the best experiences of your life.

Not all toys are created equal

It's also important to do your homework on the toys you plan to use. This is important as there is any number of toys out there. Some are rather straightforward, while others come in a variety of shapes, sizes, colors, textures, and functions. You can't really know what works for you until you try them out. So, it's always best to start off with the basics and move on from there. This is especially true when you haven't experimented with toys before. When you go about purchasing your first sex toys, you might be tempted to make a big splash. However, you might not want to spend any big bucks until you are sure what's best for you. In fact, for most folks, simple works best. So, dishing out a pretty penny for the fanciest toys may not be the best choice, at least not at first.

Getting over the mental hang up

If you have no qualms about bringing toys into the bedroom, along with your partner, then make the most of your opportunity to enjoy a pleasurable experience with your partner… and some added stimulation.

However, if you are on the fence about bringing in toys, then it's worth going over the worst-case scenario. When you really think about it, what's the worst that can happen? If you really trust your partner, then there should be no reason why toys would get in the way. For instance, if you choose to try something out, but realize that it's not for you, or it didn't work the way you expected it to, then you can simply chalk it up to experience. If anything, it could be that you haven't chosen the right one.

Please keep in mind that this chapter isn't meant to convince you to use toys. It's meant to convince you to try new things. When you are truly committed to exploring the depths of tantra, you need to be prepared to open yourself up to new experiences. Otherwise, you will never get out of your comfort zone. As such, you may never be able to truly surrender yourself to your partner and the depths of pleasure that can emerge from liberating your hang-ups. When you let go of your hang-ups, you are truly free to be yourself!

Chapter 8: Exercises During Tantric Sex

Thus far, we have focused on the various factors that make tantric sex the best sexual experience of your life. It may seem like a big claim to make. But when you really think about it, all the time and effort you have put into learning about tantra makes it truly possible.

That is why this section is devoted to specific exercises that you can use to help you achieve the heights of sexual pleasure and ecstasy you seek to achieve. As we have mentioned throughout this book, ecstasy isn't something that happens automatically. There is a certain number of elements that go into sex before you can truly hit the heights you seek.

In this chapter, we are going to focus on exercises that you can both do solo and with your partner. Ultimately, these exercises are meant to help you stimulate your own sexual energy and that of your partner. In the end, you will find these exercises to be quite simple and very enjoyable.

Going solo

First of all, let's take a look at exercises you can do solo. These exercises are great when you don't have a partner. They are also very effective when you do have a partner. The key thing about solo exercises is that you are on your own meaning that there is no pressure to perform for anyone else. These are exercises which are yours and yours alone. So, there is no going wrong. If you find that you're not quite getting what you want out of it, then keep trying. In fact, you may find these exercises worth trying on your partner later on. It could even make for a nice surprise.

When going solo, the end game isn't always masturbation. Most people have the false assumption that anything that involves touching yourself, in any way, is about masturbation. However, this could not be farther from the truth. The exercises we are going to reveal are about self-exploration. They are about getting yourself in the right condition so that you can channel your sexual energy in a positive and meaningful manner.

Solo exercise #1: Meditation

Yes, meditation. While this isn't traditionally considered to be a "sexual" exercise, it is a must if you are really focused on mastering tantra.

In this exercise, you are focusing your mind on your energy, your sensations, and the overall arousal you feel. This will help you to explore the emotions and sensations you feel during arousal. Moreover, you can use your mind's eye to help you picture the outcome you want in a sexual relationship.

Here is a great exercise you can put into practice right away:

Find a comfortable position. This could be lying on your back in your bed or perhaps on a comfy sofa—the more comfortable the position, the better. Now, begin the exercise by breathing slowly. Inhale and exhale to the full capacity of your lungs. As you fill your lungs, picture the air entering your body. Once your lungs are full, hold your breath for about 3 seconds and then exhale. Repeat this breathing exercise as many times as you like. Don't keep count as that will only serve to distract you.

Next, picture your energy flowing through your body. Picture your sexual energy building up and coursing through every fiber of your body. If you feel slightly aroused, that's perfectly normal. Try to focus on your breathing and your energy. As you feel the energy flowing, imagine how it feeds your body. Picture how it is nourishing your cells.

Try to hold this state for as long as you can. At first, this state may only last a few minutes. As you gain more practice, you might find yourself in this position for quite a long time. Don't worry if you happen to fall asleep. Sometimes, you might be tired and stressed out. So, this type of exercise gives you a profound state of relaxation, thereby causing you to fall asleep.

Solo exercise #2: Self-massaging

Self-massaging is about exploring your own body. It's about understanding every part of your body, and in particular, the areas of your body that are most susceptible to arousal. While everyone can be aroused by touching the same areas (such as the genitals), it is also true that different folks find different parts of their bodies susceptible to pleasure. That is why this exercise is about exploring your own body. After all, if you don't know what feels good, how can you expect your partner to figure it out? Sure, they will eventually, but you can shorten the learning curve by guiding your partner.

In this exercise, start out by relaxing in a comfortable position. You can undress if you like, wear a bathrobe, or perhaps stay in your underwear. The idea is to find whatever makes your most comfortable. Then, begin by breathing just like in the previous exercise. As you relax, start by touching yourself slowly and softly. Try to get a feeling for every part of your body. Don't hold back.

As you make your way around your body, try to take in the sensations produced. You may be surprised to find that some parts are more sensitive to others. Make a note of which areas are more sensitive. Try to focus on how everything feels. If you find yourself having erotic thoughts, try your best to steer your mind back to what you are actually feeling.

One great addition to this exercise is the use of oils and lotions. These can help make your touching smoother while adding a pleasant scent. Play music if you like or use other scents such as essential oils, incense, and so on. However, try to refrain from any visual stimulation as the idea is to help you see with your other senses and not just your eyes.

Solo exercise #3: Masturbation

The intention of this exercise is not to just get off. It's about exploring pleasure and what makes you feel truly satisfied. As such, rushing orgasm is not the best way to go about it. In this exercise, the main focus is to take your time to explore your genitals and all those sensitive areas of your body.

Don't hold back!

Remember, you are alone. So, there is no one judging what you are doing. This can give you the freedom to explore all areas of your body. The worst that can happen is you find something you don't really like. Nevertheless, it's worth exploring every inch of your body.

You can set the mood just like the previous two exercises. In fact, you can do these exercises in sequence. First, start off with some meditation, then some self-massaging before masturbation.

Please bear in mind that the ultimate goal is not orgasm. The ultimate goal is to manage your sensations so that you can control your arousal.

This is especially important in men. By going slow and managing your arousal, men can get more control over ejaculation, thereby prolonging the time of intercourse. As for women, this is a perfect opportunity to find what type of stimulation works best in pursuit of the big "O." Oh, and by the way, use toys if you wish!

Working with a partner

These exercises are intended to help you and your partner find the right combination of stimulation, intimacy, pleasure, and arousal. While that may sound like a great deal of things in one package, the truth is that all of these elements interact together in a single cycle. So, when you hit one target, that activates the next and so on.

So, here are three great exercises you can try with your partner:

Team exercise #1: Foreplay

There is a lot about foreplay in sexual literature. In fact, we have talked extensively about foreplay in this book. However, we haven't honed in on a couple of aspects that are essential to tantric sex.

Please bear in mind that foreplay is essential. It can be as long or as short as you like. There might be times when both of you are ready to go, while there may be others when a little more warming up is needed.

For this exercise, you can choose to undress, dress, wear costumes, lingerie, whatever hits the spot for you. Also, you can lie in bed, sit on a sofa, stand in the kitchen, be in the car (somewhere that isn't too public), or anywhere you can find the privacy and intimacy that you seek.

First, by syncing your breathing. You can use the same breathing technique we presented in solo exercise one. Now, take the time to look at each other. Explore each other's bodies with your eyes. Try to take in every aspect of your partner's body. Then, begin by touching. You can use lotion or oil if you wish. This isn't just a massage; it's touching that's meant to arouse you. As the energy builds, you can take turns touching each other, especially in those areas where you feel most sensitive. Don't forget to kiss your partner as much as you like.

At this point, you can take things to the next level. Here, you can make use of toys, or perhaps oral stimulation. If you choose, you can take turns stimulating one another. Or, you might choose to stimulate each other at the same time. Anything goes!

Please bear in mind that the point of this exercise is not sex per se. The point is to build arousal and intimacy in such a way that both of you learn what truly turns you on. In fact, you may choose to avoid sexual intercourse and perhaps bring about orgasm through the use of toys, fingers, oral, and manual stimulation. The fact is that there is nothing carved in stone. If you wish, you can have sex and make it the full package.

Team exercise #2: Snuggling or cuddling

Earlier, we described this exercise as a means of fostering intimacy. In this variation, we are going to spice things up so that it can be used as foreplay, or just as a means of stimulating arousal.

To carry out this position, we are going to be "spooning." This is a position in which both partners lie on their sides. Then, the partner that is behind the other holds the other. This creates a "giver" and "receiver."

With this exercise, you can take it as far as you like. You can lie there breathing in sync or take it up a notch. For instance, you can undress and touch. The giver takes the time to explore the receiver thereby arousing and stimulating them. If this leads to sex, then the "spoon" position is there for your enjoyment. Or, you may choose to engage in or oral or manual stimulation.

Please bear in mind that this exercise isn't intended to lead to sex. It's about getting you to feel comfortable with each other's bodies so that sex becomes that much more potent.

Team exercise #3: Sex

Traditional sex is defined as intercourse, that is, penetration of some kind. Well, this isn't traditional sex. In this exercise, "sex" is anything you want it to be. In fact, you can even mix things up. Some couples feel the need for penetration every time they have sex. Other couples use penetration as the final act following the exercises outlined in this chapter. Other couples use penetration as a lead into other events such as oral or manual stimulation. And then, there are toys…

After you have truly become comfortable with your partner, sex becomes a natural occurrence that stems from stimulation and arousal. In fact, you don't really think about "sex" when you are with your partner. All you think about is enjoying your time with them. Then, things can go any way you want them, too. The main thing is to be on the same page and enjoy your encounter. That is the bottom line. Whatever you choose to do at this point, please bear in mind that giving is just as good as receiving. So, if you feel compelled to take turns, then so be it. If you feel compelled to reach the big "O" together, then you can take your time to work yourselves up to that point.

Chapter 9: Positions During Tantric Sex

Much is written about positions in tantric sex. However, most of what you will find is a collection of various positions that don't really espouse the philosophy of tantric sex. Sure, it might be fun to try a different configuration. But at the end of the day, if your head is not into the tantric frame of mind, then the positions you try will not lead you to the ultimate ecstasy you are seeking.
With that in mind, this chapter is about taking sex positions that are a staple of tantric sex so that you can incorporate them into your own sex life right away. Sure, you may have tried them before, it's a guarantee that you haven't tried them like this before.
So, try to keep an open mind in this chapter. Now, you may not be surprised by these positions, but when you see the spin that we have put on them, you will regret no having tried this sooner!

Going on the power play

This might sound like you're playing hockey, but the power play is all about that, "power."
In this position, we're not really talking about intertwining your bodies in one manner or the other. It's about giving your partner free rein to do what they like with you. By surrendering your power, you allow your partner to take you to places you may not have been to before.
But first a disclaimer: when trying out the power play, it's important to talk about boundaries. For instance, you might say that anything in the backdoor is off-limits. Also, make a point of telling your partner what you like best. By the same token, pay attention to what drives your partner crazy. It could be that you already know how to push all of the right buttons.
That being said, the power play isn't anything like BDSM (unless you're actually into it). This is more about letting go. For instance, the use of blindfolds or masks is highly useful. The idea is that when you cancel out senses, you force the others to make up for it. Thus, your heightened sensitivity makes you feel pleasure in a whole new level.

Here is a simple yet effective angle on the powerplay.

Let's assume you are giving pleasure. Lay your partner down on their back. Use a blindfold, sleeping mask, or any other means of blocking their sight. Now, slowly undress your partner. Do it in such a way that they can anticipate your movements. The only rule is that they can't move or push you away. If you feel inclined to use handcuffs or any other type of restraint, then by all means. Now, as you approach the genital area, slowly caress their inner thigh.

At this point, you have two options. One, you can continue the caressing and proceed to masturbate your partner. In the case of a man, slowly stroking the penis will not only cause a great deal of pleasure but will allow him to control his need to ejaculate. Use lubrication if you like. In the case of a woman, stimulating the clitoris can be a great way to get things rolling. You can then choose to take your partner all the way to orgasm, or perhaps use this exercise as a warm-up.

The second option is to perform oral pleasure on your partner. The same rules apply here. You can work your way slowly so that the sensation is that much stronger. You can take your partner all the way to orgasm, or just use it as a means of setting the stage.

One of the great things about this technique is that you can use it as a means of controlling orgasm. For men, it's a great way to help control the urge to ejaculate. The trick is to get close to the "point of no return" before settling back down again. In the case of women, building up "pressure" so to speak, can lead to a massive "O." Other women may feel inclined to just have multiple orgasms as a result of oral or manual stimulation, or both.

Also, the use of toys is perfectly fine here. Just make sure that you are on the same page about the toys to be used and how they are meant to be used.

Take things slow

Throughout this book, we have talked about the importance of going slow. This is very important when you are starting out with tantra. Please bear in mind that this isn't about how hard and fast you can go. If anything, tantra is about taking things slow and relishing every moment with your partner.

At first, it's a great idea to start out with traditional positions such as the missionary and the cowgirl (or reverse if you like). With the missionary, the male is on top of the female. Now, it's important to resist the urge to go fast. Rather, the goal here is to go slow. Ideally, slow, deep penetration works really well.

Here's a simple way of ensuring this position works wonders. Count to 4. Yes, that's right. Start out with three shorter, shallower thrusts and one deep, hard thrust. The fourth thrust should last just a little bit longer than the first three. This technique will allow you to get into a rhythm. Please bear in mind that tantra is all about finding a rhythm. When you get into that rhythm, then the female can experience a rather predictable outcome: a big "O."

In the case of the cowgirl (or reverse cowgirl), the female is on top. As such, the female is in control of the movement. So, it's a great idea to play the same 4-count: three shallow thrusts and one deep, prolonged thrust. This will allow the female to control the sensation thereby enabling a rhythmic movement.

You will find that even though these are very traditional positions, they really work very well when you are able to build a rhythm. Eventually, both of you will be able to sync everything, movement, breathing, and eye contact. If you choose to cancel sight, then breathing becomes highly important in order to ensure you are on the same page.

The final lap

This is the classic tantric sex position. In this one, the man sits upright, preferably with his back up against something firm for support, legs stretched out (not crossed). Then, the woman sits on his lap. The woman's legs should wrap around the man's buttocks. Kneeling is not recommended as it can get quite tiring very quickly. She can then wrap her arms around the man's neck or use her hands to caress him. The man can also wrap his arms around the woman or use his hands to caress her.

This is a very intimate position as it always for a number of things. First, kissing is the go-to option here. Also, it's great for breathing exercises. You can simply hold each other and attempt to sync your breathing. In addition, you can caress each other in unison. For instance, massaging each other's backs, buttocks and chest are all good exercises.

The other great thing about this position is that you can achieve penetration with it. So, if you want to take it up a notch, then it's certainly an option. One interesting thing about this position is that due to its nature, you can't move very fast. So, it's ideal for tantra. Plus, the level of intimacy you can achieve with this position is excellent.

The reverse lap

This position is essentially the same as the previous with a twist: one of the partners sits with their back to the wall while the other sits on their lap but with their back facing their partner. As such, the first partner only sees the back of the second. The second partner is essentially the recipient of the former's attention.

When engaging in this position, the first partner essentially has access to the second partner. They can caress just about every part of their partner's body while having the option of kissing the back of their neck, shoulders, and upper back.

One of the great things about this position is that you can switch things up. So, the man can hold the female, or the female can hold the male. So, it's great for taking turns and pampering each other. If you choose to penetrate, the female can sit on the man's lap and do so. At this point, the position works pretty much like a reverse cowgirl. And just like the previous position, there's not much room to move fast. So, you really don't have much choice but to take it slow.

One very nice variation of this position is that it can be done in a bathtub, jacuzzi, or a swimming pool. If you're in public, well, you have to keep it civil. But in private, you can take it up as far as you want to. A bubble bath is one of the go-to moves for this position.

Spooning

Earlier, we talked about how spooning can be a great tool for fostering intimacy. In this case, it's also a great position for having intercourse. Additionally, it works really well because you can't move very fast even if you wanted to. Spooning can work both ways as the female can hold the male and vice-versa. If you are intent on penetration, then it works very well, especially because it favors syncing your movements. Plus, it's one of the most intimate positions you will find in the tantric sex toolkit.

The other great thing about spooning is that it can be quite erotic without necessarily leading to sex. It's good for syncing breathing and it's also good for post-sex cuddling. In fact, lots of couples love sleeping like this. So, that's an added bonus.

One other twist to spooning is the ability to masturbate your partner. This works well if you're keen on pleasuring your partner. In fact, you can practice syncing up your breathing while masturbating your partner. As you can see, it's the position that keeps on giving!

Mutual masturbation

On the subject of touching, mutual masturbation is a great way of syncing everything up. This technique works well to sync breathing, practice eye contact, and also kissing passionately. So, let's take a look at a couple of ways in which you could make this work.

The first is by both partners lying on their backs. Then touching ensues. But the key here is that the touching needs to be at the same speed. If one goes faster than the other, you might get a big "O" ahead of time. Also, it might be a bit hard to focus when your partner is going at a different rate than you are.

Another position is lying on your side, facing one another. This position allows you to make eye contact, kiss, and basically have access to the entire front part of your partner's body. This variation is great if you are just looking to lie in bed, spend some time together, and throw in a fun ending.

The third variation to sit, facing each other. For this one, both partners sit upright on the same surface. So, one does not sit on the lap of the other. This variation is great for eye contact and breathing. It also allows you both to touch each other slowly. Given the nature of the position, you can't go very fast. That is a great thing in the world of tantra, of course.

So, there you have some great position which you can practice today. Please keep in mind that anything goes in tantra. You can do any of the positions you enjoy. However, the ones we have presented in this chapter are intended to help you get into the rhythm of tantra. Eventually, you'll be able to mix things up as suits your mood.

Chapter 10: Massages During Tantric Sex

Massaging has to be the most recognizable part of tantric sex. All experts on the topic recommend the use of massaging as a means of engaging in tantra. However, not too many experts take the time to explain while massaging is such a useful tactic when it comes to tantric sex.

The main reason behind massaging's effectiveness is that it promotes a sensory response that other techniques don't really provide. This is important as tantra is based, first and foremost, on sensory perception. After all, traditional sex is "traditional" because it's just about finding the quickest way to orgasm.

When you take the time to practice massage, you will discover a two-way street that you had no idea already existed. First, the incredible sensation that comes with receiving a tantric massage. The second, the unbelievable satisfaction that comes with giving your partner a tremendous experience. Both of these situations can leave you feeling both satisfied and nurtured.

Massaging roles

Basically, there are two roles in tantric massaging, the giver and receiver. The giver is the person performing the massage while the receiver is the one who is the recipient of the massage. Both roles are important in tantra as each partner connects to the other, thus producing the tantric experience.

If you are more inclined to a dominant or submissive role, massaging provides a great opportunity to feed this side. For example, more dominant individuals can take their partners into their hands, literally, and give them an extraordinary experience. If you are a more submissive person, then you can fully surrender yourself in your partner's touch.

However, massaging is also great at inverting the power dynamic. More predominantly submissive individuals can take the opportunity to be in the lead. They can give their dominant partner some much-deserved attention and pampering. The dominant partner has the chance to relinquish power for a short while. This can be a refreshing change that can help a dominant individual get away from their comfort zone to find a different role in the relationship.

Massaging also allows each partner to take turns. It's a bit hard to massage each other at the same time. So, the best way to go about it is to just take turns. Now, it can be hard to receive a massage, pop up, and then give one. As such, you might work out a deal in which one receives a massage on one occasion and then the other on the next occasion.

Still, taking turns can work well if you plan on simpler things like a shoulder rub or foot massage (this is awesome if you have a foot fetish). So, do make time for massaging as part of your love life. If you haven't given it a try, you'll regret not having done it sooner.

Setting the stage

Setting the stage for a massage is highly important. If you are keen on pulling out all the stops, a massage table is the best way to go. Alternatively, just lying in bed is great. Lying on a couch also works, but because of the design of couches, it can be a bit tough to access all of your partner's body.

Scented candles, essential oils, or incense are great ways of providing a pleasant smell. Soft music, nature sounds, or some smooth jazz can also enhance the mood. Visuals are important too, such as dim lighting or perhaps candlelight.

One very important aspect of setting the stage is to minimize distractions. This means blocking out the world around you. Please keep in mind that both the giver and receiver ought to focus on the events as they are happening. So, eliminating distractions is a must.

An interesting twist could be to massage your partner in a tub or jacuzzi. You can make use of bath salts to create a pleasant atmosphere. This works exceptionally well when you are looking to alleviate stress. Water has a great way of making aches and pains go away. Plus, massages in water tend to be a lot more intimate than say in bed or massage table.

Using equipment

This largely depends on what you are going for. You can keep things very simple by just using your hands and some oil. There are various types of oil that you can use on your partner. The most common type of oil is regular baby oil. It serves as a very nice lubricant while also stimulating the skin. There is also a wide range of massage oils. Some are scented while others vary in texture. So, it's up to you to experiment with whatever you feel would work best for you.

Additionally, if you are inclined to use any sex toys, feel free to bring them into the mix (more on that in a minute). Any other props such as mallets, rubber balls, or vibrators could enhance the experience. In a way, massaging is about trial and error. This means that you can try out various things and see what works best for you. If you find that one thing doesn't work, then you can just move on from it.

A good piece of advice here is to avoid rushing out to buy a bunch of massage gear. Start out with your hands and move on from there. The best equipment which you can use is your hands!

The proper technique

When using tantric massage, the question of the "proper technique" comes to mind. Often, folks are unsure about whether to rub, or stroke, or do karate chops. The fact of the matter is that you don't need to be a professional massage therapist to give your partner a pleasurable experience. In fact, you can just start out by running your hands down your partner's limbs, back, and shoulder. In addition, the use of oils can greatly reduce the amount of friction when rubbing your partner down. So, that creates the warm sensation of being touched while also allowing yourself to control the movements you are doing.

One interesting spin is to take a couple's massage class. In this type of class, a trained professional shows you how to rub down your partner. So, it's not them doing the rubbing; it's you, but with the guidance of a pro. For couples looking to build an intimate experience, this class actually works really well despite having a third person in the room with you.

Alternatively, online tutorials can help you get a good sense of what to do and how to handle your partner. In fact, watching such tutorials can even create arousal. In a manner of speaking, it provides a great visual.

With that in mind, here is a great four-step plan you can put into practice right away.

First, let's start with relaxation. To get ready for a massage, you can practice breathing with your partner. The receiver lies down on their back while the giver sets the pace for breathing. The giver can begin by providing light caresses on the legs, arms, or just simply being there.

Next, as relaxation sets in, work your way up. To do this, begin by providing a foot rub, working your way up on the calves, shins, and thighs. You don't need any particular technique here. Basically, all you need is light rubbing with your hands or the oil of your choice. Lotion works well, too.

After, try to avoid the genital area at this point. While you might be tempted to go for it, it's best to wait until you have completed the entire body massage. While you might have a happy ending for your partner in mind, the main point of the tantric massage is to foster intimacy and give your partner the best experience. As such, you can caress their inner thigh, eventually working your way up their stomach, chest, and down their arms.

Once you have reached the shoulders, ask your partner to flip over on to their belly. Now, you can work your way down their back to their buttocks and the back of their legs. At this point, you can focus on their thighs. Here, you can decide to stimulate the genital area if you wish. You can ask your partner to flip back on to their back to focus on their genital area.

Lastly, it's important to be aware of what the point of the massage is. If you want to use the massage as a means of foreplay prior to sexual intercourse, then certainly stimulating your partner's genital area serves the purpose. You can use your hands or even perform oral pleasure. The use of toys can also work here.

If the point of the massage is not sexual per se, then you can leave it at that. Please bear in mind that if you are not planning on any sexual activity as it relates to the massage, then make this clear to your partner, so there are no expectations. However, the chances are that you may not resist and choose to take it further.

Happy ending?

This question always comes up when discussing tantric massages. In general, you can provide your partner with a happy ending if you are both comfortable with it. This is important to note, as you may not be comfortable with this idea at first. Generally speaking, the giver may feel left out if the receiver orgasms while they don't receive any reciprocal pleasure.

One of the deals you can make it to take turns. You can choose to pamper your partner one day while you are in line for the next round. Otherwise, you could take turns massaging one another before sexual activity.

The fact of the matter is that massages provide you with the opportunity to foster both intimacy and to pamper your partner. Please bear in mind that one of the core tenets is to provide your partner with the attention they seek. By the same token, you should also be on the receiving end. This is why we have stated throughout this book that tantra is a two-way street. Of course, communication is the key in this regard.

What to watch out for

While tantric massages are more about providing your partner with an experience that goes beyond the actual massage technique you are using, it's worth mentioning that you and your partner should communicate on what feels good and what you enjoy most. For instance, you might have highly sensitive areas. As such, your partner needs to be aware of this. Likewise, you need to be aware of which areas are sensitive to your partner.

Also, setting a time and place for massages is key. While that may sound mechanical (like having to set an appointment) the fact is that improvising a massage session may not provide you with the results you seek. This is why many tantra practitioners make time for themselves and their partners. Since you want to dedicate as much time and attention as you can to the occasion, making time for your partner is a must.

On the whole, tantric massage is a technique that evolves among partners. Over time, you will find what works for both of you. Then, you can take that knowledge and translate it into an experience which makes sense for both you. That way, your massage sessions will become as pleasurable as they can become. If this leads to sex, then so be it. If it doesn't lead to sex, then it's still a wonderful experience that can set the stage for further sessions.

Please keep in mind that tantra isn't necessarily about sex. This misconception tends to permeate the minds of folks all over. When you see that tantra is just the overarching theme that also happens to include sex, you will find that your overall feelings about your sex life and your relationship with your partner change drastically.

So, make the time for yourself and your partner. You won't regret prioritizing this part of your life.

Chapter 11: What is Tantric Pleasure?

Pleasure is the most talked-about aspect regarding tantra. After all, what point would there be to tantra is there wasn't any pleasure involved?

The fact of the matter is pleasure is the core of the entire tantra practice. Pleasure is of the utmost importance. So, that's why we are going to have an in-depth discussion on pleasure and what it means to give it and receive it.

As we have stated numerous times in this book, tantra is a two-way street. As such, tantra is both about giving and receiving. Unlike other approaches in which students are taught to either give or receive pleasure, tantra is about reciprocity. This means that you should get as much as you give and vice-versa. If you feel that you are giving more than you get, then something is not entirely right. Good tantra practice means that you are able to feel as satisfied as your partner.

What is tantric pleasure?

Now, the question begs: what is pleasure?

Generally speaking, pleasure is a feeling of goodness in your physical body. This feeling is the result of engaging in a pleasurable sexual activity. The degree of pleasure that you are able to feel depends on your partner, the activities you do, and your ability to actually feel pleasure.

This is important as there are many folks out there who have trouble feeling pleasure. A common issue with feeling pleasure is generally associated with the feelings you might have about the activities in which you are engaging. For some, sex is synonymous with impure activities. For others, they may feel guilty about feeling pleasure.

While it is not our intention to explore the causes of being unable to feel pleasure, we are looking to establish that pleasure is about feeling good when engaging in sexual activity. Pleasure derived from traditional sex is limited to the physical body. This means that you are able to feel pleasure though it doesn't go beyond a temporary feeling of satisfaction.

For men, pleasure is generally derived from penetration or oral stimulation. For women, pleasure is also derived from penetration or oral stimulation though it should be noted that there is an emotional component that also provides pleasure. In addition, sensory experience also produces pleasure. Visual stimulation is key while olfactory and auditory stimulation also plays a key role. On the whole, you should strive to combine as many senses as possible during sexual encounters. This will enhance the overall feeling of pleasure derived from the sexual act itself.

Yet, we haven't defined "tantric pleasure."

Tantric pleasure is the result of feeling pleasure at a physical, emotional, and even spiritual level. This type of pleasure is the result of your ability to connect on a deep level with your partner. As such, you are not merely finding physical gratification. You are entering a realm of profound connection that goes beyond the mere physical encounter.

When you hit this level, you are not only satisfying the physical, instinctive desire, but you are also nourishing your spiritual and emotional need for connection. When you really think about it, this is why many folks say they are left with an empty feeling after sex.

What's the reason?

The lack of emotional connection with their partner!

Now, you could develop a strong, emotional connection with someone you've just met. This can happen simply based on the fact that you have an open mind. In other words, you are open to communicating with someone on a deeper level. While this isn't something that happens with everyone you meet, it is something that can certainly happen when you know what you are looking for.

All about physical pleasure

The first step to tantric pleasure is physical. This is the starting point. As such, we can't ignore this point. In fact, if you try to skip physical pleasure and go straight to an emotional connection, you are missing a very important component. Physical pleasure is vital as this is what fosters the overall enjoyment of the sexual encounter. Even though it's true that you can have a tantric experience without sexual intercourse, there is still a strong physical component. For example, when you have a tantric massage, there is a strong physical connection. Just the fact that you are doing the massage is enough to get you to really feel good at a physical level.

Also, physical pleasure is vital is generating the positive energies that course through your body. Without it, it would be very hard to achieve a sense of wellness. The key here is that there is a clear mind-body-spirit connection. So, you cannot ignore the physical. It is important and must be given its proper place. Another important aspect of physical pleasure is the sensory experience that goes with a tantric session. You see, we perceive the world around us through our senses. As such, we can't expect to have a full tantric experience without being cognizant of the role our senses play. In this regard, setting the scene is pivotal in ensuring that you, and your partner, get the most out of your experience.

Establishing an emotional connection

As far as emotional connections go, it's not always easy to develop one. If you have ever been with a person in which your relationship did not involve any kind of feelings, then you can appreciate how empty this type of relationship can be. When you are devoid of emotional connections, you can't fully appreciate the level of passion between two people.

That is why tantra focuses heavily on developing intimacy. As we have stated on several occasions, tantra is not necessarily about sex. It's about creating an emotional connection through intimacy, which can bring you and your partner together. When you make a point of executing the exercises we have presented, you can build intimacy with your partner at a very deep level. Please bear in mind that intimacy is built on trust. When you build trust, you can create a feeling in which you are certain that every encounter with your partner will be a memorable one. Even if there is no sex involved, you can be sure that it will make your life that much more enjoyable.

Emotional connections are also built outside of the bedroom. The overall tantric experience can carry over into your everyday life. If you are in a committed relationship, you can see how the small things truly add up. For instance, showing genuine concern for your partner breeds the type of trust that cannot be easily matched. In addition, your attention and devotion to your partner will signify how much they mean to you.

Does that mean you need to spend every waking moment with them?

Of course not.

But it does mean that the time you devote to them must count. There is no point in spending time with them for the sake of spending time, as this will not foster the type of relationship you are looking to build. That is why your dedication to building intimacy is crucial when it comes to tantra.

Here is an important reflection on intimacy: intimacy is a hard thing to build. It generally takes a long time to build, but it can be easily destroyed. Your actions can quickly undermine the intimacy you have worked hard to build. This is why it's always recommended that you, and your partner, take the time to work out any unresolved issues between you. Such issues create a wedge in between you. So, it's best to get them out of the way so that there is nothing lurking in the shadows.

Building a spiritual connection

Once you have built a strong physical connection and a deep emotional bond, you can then move on to building a spiritual connection. This connection is not easily attained. It is generally the result of trust and understanding. That is why you can't expect to skip a physical and emotional connection in order to get to a spiritual connection.

However, there is a "chicken or the egg" dilemma that arises when considering spiritual connections. Does the spiritual connection happen first, and that leads to a physical connection, or does the physical connection happen first, and that leads to the spiritual connection?

This dilemma can be answered in the following manner:

It depends on the circumstances.

There are times when two people have an instant physical attraction. This is commonly called "chemistry." So, when you see two people have chemistry, they quickly develop a strong physical bond. This bond may be expanded to include an emotional component. For instance, a purely physical relationship can develop into a romance. This romantic nature is when people "fall in love." Thus, it should be noted that falling in love is a question of a deep emotional bond that cannot be cast aside. Then, the relationship may evolve into a deeper spiritual connection. This is commonly seen in those couples who claim to know what their partner is thinking. Such relationships are rare but do provide an interesting point of view on going from a physical to a spiritual connection.

The flip side of this question is when two people are drawn to each other for some mysterious reason. This can be seen in the way "opposites attract," or someone has that "X factor." When you see these relationships, there is a deeper bond that cannot be easily ignored. The spiritual bond can then evolve into a deeper emotional and then physical connection. The end result is a platonic relationship that morphs into a physical one.

In either of these cases, there is a logical process in which the two parties move through a natural progression. It's not the type of thing in which you are hitting things off one day, and then deeply in love the next. Also, you can't expect to admire someone for immaterial reasons and then jump in the sack with them. There has to be a natural progression through the various stages of a deep and meaningful relationship. Granted, there are times when things happen very quickly. However, it's not the type of thing that can happen overnight.

Using tantra as a means of deepening connections

Can tantra be used to help a couple progress through the various stages of a relationship?

We thought you'd never ask!

Tantra is perfect for helping couples go from one stage of their relationship with another. In particular, tantra can help those couples that have been in a relationship for a while but seem to have lost that spark. As such, it's a great way or rekindling that passion that may have been lost over the years. As a matter of fact, tantra has been known to help couples rediscover each other in ways that they may have forgotten. If this sounds like you, then you must try tantra right away.

In the event that you are in a new relationship, tantra can help you settle into a dynamic in which you can go about discovering everything about one another. It can help you set the tone for your relationship moving forward. As a matter of fact, it's a great way of bonding especially if you've had negative experiences in the past. Tantra can deepen the bond between you while also helping you find a balance between the physical and the spiritual. If you are single, then take this opportunity to wrap your mind around the tantra philosophy. You will find that being alone gives you a good opportunity to assess the situation you are in and make any changes you see fit moving forward. That will enable you to become the best version of yourself. That way, when you are ready to be in a relationship, you can make the most of your time with your new partner.
What could be better than that?

Chapter 12: The Male Orgasm

In a nutshell, the male orgasm is commonly associated with ejaculation. There would be no need to write any more about it if we kept this narrow perspective. However, when we take a broader perspective on this subject, we can see that orgasm and ejaculation are two completely different concepts. Yes, they are linked; however, they are not mutually bound to one another. This implies that men can have orgasms, multiple orgasms even, without the need to ejaculate.

If this is something that surprises you, then you might be surprised to find that an orgasm is not necessarily a physiological response to sexual arousal. Rather, it is an electrochemical reaction in the brain, which triggers the sensation of pleasure. How does this work?

In order to fully understand how the male orgasm works, it's important to understand the entire dynamic that goes on within the male body and how this pertains to the ultimate climax of pleasure.

How arousal works

Men are predominantly visual creatures. This is the direct result of evolution. The male brain evolved in accordance with the needs and the environment in which early humans developed. Since the traditional male role was that of hunter-gatherer, the male brain developed a much broader set of skills related to vision. Consequently, males are much more inclined toward visuals rather than other senses, such as hearing.

Over the centuries, this visual nature has not diminished. Men are still predominantly visual. This is why many of the typically male professions deal with the measurement of distance and space in addition to calculations of speed, volume, mass, and so on. While this doesn't mean that women cannot do these professions, men are more biologically suited for them.

That being said, arousal in males is typically a visual event. Therefore, males are far more attracted to a visually esthetic female than females would be to a visually attractive male. As such, males tend to focus on a certain set of features that are considered to be attractive. For example, males find a youthful look much more appealing as it signals an instinctive reaction indicating that the female is apt for procreation.

When attraction, at a physical level, takes place, the brain signals the body to start moving blood flow to the genital area. To do this, the heart needs to work a little bit harder to ensure that blood flow is sufficient. In addition, the heart works harder, but blood vessels also need to widen in order to accommodate the increased blood flow. This is what eventually leads to an erection.

Now, let's assume that sex is about to take place. While arousal is happening, there is no sensation of pleasure yet. After all, if there is no "action," then there cannot be any presence of pleasure. This is where traditional sex gets it wrong.

In traditional sexual culture, men are taught to stimulate their genital area in such a way that pleasurable sensations are sent throughout the body; the brain decodes it and floods the body with feel-good chemicals such as endorphins. However, when the arousal stage moves into actual sex, if there is no control over the psychological aspects of the event, then what you end up having is the male ejaculating. This reaction is often confused with orgasm. Yet, it is a known fact that ejaculation and orgasm are two separate phenomena.

Why?

You see, ejaculation is a physiological response that is associated with procreation. Naturally, this function has to feel good. Otherwise, why would humans procreate if sex was unpleasant? Mother nature needed to make sure that it felt good so that the species could reproduce and thrive.

With that in mind, arousal leads to orgasm when a male is able to separate ejaculation from pleasure. When a male is engaged in tantric sex, his focus is moved away from the various aspects of sexual relations to the more emotional and even spiritual aspects of it. As such, his focus is moved away from feeling good physically, to enjoying the overall experience of it.

Many tantra practitioners say that they feel a greater sense of arousal and stimulation by letting go of their physiological sensations and focusing more on the sensory experience. This includes breathing and touching. Also, very powerful emotions are unleashed when males are able to focus on their partner's pleasure in addition to their own.

Getting to the big "O."

At this point, the big "O" becomes a question of the brain being able to process the sensory perception in such a way that it releases massive amounts of endorphins (among other substances) into the bloodstream. There is a cocktail of brain chemicals such as adrenaline and serotonin. The interaction of the chemicals in the brain leads to the overall feeling of pleasure. However, the interaction of these chemicals leads to overloading the nervous system to the point where an incredible sensation of pleasure takes over the entire nervous system in a wave-like manner.

This is an orgasm.

Guys who feel these orgasms during sex report they feel their erections getting stronger without the need to ejaculate. While the pleasure signals are there, they are not directly linked to the overall feeling of needing to ejaculate.

This is how you can separate one thing from the other.

In theory, this sounds all well and fine. But being able to achieve it is an entirely different ballgame. The challenge here is to overcome the conditioning instilled during adolescence. In many cases, adolescent boys learn that "faster is better." Sadly, this is a tremendous disservice that is done to mean as they grow up without being able to truly enjoy sex for what it's worth.

By fostering the erroneous perception that finishing fast is the best way, men are taught to deprive themselves of the magical experience that comes with truly enjoying sex with their chosen partner. When a man is able to achieve true orgasm, there is no comparison. This is why tantra is such a seemingly mysterious art form.

The good news here is that anyone can achieve true orgasms. Best of all, any man can achieve multiple orgasms while only needing to ejaculate once. If this sounds new to you, then do read on as we will describe the steps that you can take you to achieve this.

First, it's time to dissociate orgasm and ejaculation. They are two separate concepts. Orgasms are electrochemical reactions in the brain, while ejaculation is a physiological response to arousal and stimulation. The sooner you are able to separate these concepts from your mind, the sooner you'll be able to truly enjoy the time you spend with your partner.

Next, let go of the idea that the ultimate goal of sex is… sex. Of course, the main point of sex is to engage in intercourse with your partner. However, it is focusing solely on sex that makes it hard for a man to truly enjoy the situation. Generally, there is so much pressure to "perform." As such, this creates unneeded pressure. Why would you put so much pressure on yourself to do something pleasurable? Do you put so much pressure on yourself to eat properly? If you did, you wouldn't know a bit of anything you ate.

The same goes for sex. So, take the time to enjoy and savor all of the emotions, sights, and experiences that come with being someone you are attracted to, or even someone you love. This makes the entire experience much more rewarding.

Now, when you are in the midst of intercourse with your partner, try your best to remove your mind from what you are doing. This sounds paradoxical but the fact that is that if you concentrate on "doing it," then you end up getting caught up in not finishing too soon. Plus, your mind begins to play tricks on you. You start to wonder if your partner is enjoying it or if you are doing it right. These tricks are highly detrimental to your level of satisfaction while limiting the amount of enjoyment the both of you can derive from an encounter.

This is why tantra is about slowing the pace of the game. When you slow the pace of the game, you have the option to exert more control over the situation. If you feel that you are about to lose control, you can slow things down or even stop altogether. Some men find it useful to pull out and focus on touching, kissing, and caressing their partner while things settle down. Again, if your goal is to give your partner an orgasm, then you only see half of the picture. But if your goal is to give your partner the best possible experience, then you are on the right track.

Lastly, use your mind to focus your energy. This means that you ought to use your mind to move your energy throughout your body. Imagine your energy flowing throughout your body, nourishing everything in its path. This energy not only serves as a means of charging the body, but it also serves as a means of helping your body heal and repair itself. That might seem a bit strange. However, sex is known to promote healing energy within the body.

Additionally, you can recycle that energy between you and your partner. This is an energy that you are both sharing as a result of the mutual pleasure that you are sharing. When you both take the time to really savor your encounter, you will find that the "pressure" builds up. As this pressure builds up, the release of energy is an amazing feeling, unlike anything you've felt before. These are the mind-blowing orgasms that come with tantric sex.

Making sense of male pleasure

There is nothing wrong with feeling pleasure. It's a logical consequence of sex. If you believe that feeling pleasure is somehow wrong, you are only hurting yourself insofar as depriving yourself of wonderful experiences. In addition, you are also depriving your partner of having a wonderful experience alongside you.

So, finding true tantric pleasure is about framing your mind in such a way that you can enjoy the situation by taking in all the senses. Therefore, you can't rush this process. This isn't the type of process which you can complete with an egg timer. This is the type of process in which you need to be present at the moment things are happening. If your mind is wandering off, then you can't really make it work. By the same token, if your mind is focused on "performing," then the chances of you actually enjoying your encounter is far less.

Experienced tantra practitioners know that sex isn't about keeping score. There isn't some magic number that you need to hit in order to considered "good." What you will find is that there is a threshold in which you know you are moving in the right direction. This threshold is different for everyone. Nevertheless, your partner will be quite clear in showing you where they are going. If the experience is pleasurable for them, they will surely make it obvious.

So, if you are putting pressure on yourself to perform, it's time to drop those expectations and focus on sex for what it is. Take the time to assess your expectations and bring them into perspective.

Your job, if you will, is to create an experience that your partner will thoroughly enjoy. This includes everything around you, from the scene, the sights, smells, sounds, and of course, sex. Beyond that, please keep in mind that sex is a work in progress. You can't expect to hit the heights of tantric sex right away. While the guidelines we have laid out will make an immediate impact, you can't expect to hit the heights immediately. It takes time to really click with your partner. Of course, it doesn't take years, but it does take a concerted effort to make sure that you and your partner get what you want about of your sex life.

Chapter 13: The Female Orgasm

In most literature, it seems that the female orgasm is shrouded in mystery. Some so-called experts claim that it's quite easy to find multiple orgasms. They make it seems as though there is some kind of switch you can simply flip and off you go.

Other gurus make it seem like it some kind of unattainable phenomenon that can only be uncovered by the proprietary method. As such, you stand no chance of achieving orgasm unless you follow their time-tested, patented moves.

The fact of the matter is that the female orgasm works in the same way that the male orgasm does. The female orgasm is an electrochemical reaction that releases all of the chemicals that produce the wonderful feelings that come with having a good time in bed.

However, it is also important to point out that the road to the female orgasm is different. Even if the overall reaction is the same for both men and women, getting there is a bit different. This means that you need to focus on the various components that lead up to the big "O."

In this chapter, we are going to be focusing on the elements which lead up to that big "O." In particular, we're going to be discussing the main reasons why reaching orgasm can be difficult. With the ideas that we will present, you'll be able to get a much broader perspective on the limitations that you may be encountering.

Arousal in women

Unlike men, women are not predominantly visual. Yes, women find visual stimulation highly enjoyable. Women value the visual esthetics of an attractive individual as much as men do. The difference is that women do not value visual attractiveness above everything else. In fact, women tend to value visual symmetry a lot more than men do.

When talking about symmetry, it's important to keep in mind that women enjoy men who look proportionate. That is why most women don't find bodybuilders particularly attractive. The same goes for men who are too thin or those who are obese. The secret is maintaining a proportionate look in terms of height and weight. This means that while men don't need a chiseled body to be attractive, trying to maintain proper proportions makes a huge difference.

The way arousal works in women is that you have an overall sensory experience that leads to a set of emotions. It is this emotional connection between sex and emotions that leads to a pleasant sexual experience. In a manner of speaking, if your heart is not into it, then arousal can be hard to pursue.

Of course, there is instinctive arousal which is mainly driven by the need for physical intimacy. However, this need for physical intimacy is often confused with sex. Sadly, culture has reduced intimacy with sex. The reality is that sex is only one part of intimacy. This is why we have made a strong case for the need to incorporate intimacy in your life without making sex the main priority. When you take the need for sex out of the equation, you are left with the entire scene around you. When this scene isn't there, then you have no choice but to build it.

Fostering arousal should then become about creating a safe atmosphere in which you feel comfortable being yourself. Now, this is crucial as feeling uncomfortable, in any way, can be a huge detrimental factor in limiting your ability to truly enjoy sex. When you feel comfortable with yourself and everything you are doing, then you can certainly make things work as best as it can for you.

What's holding you back

Inexperienced individuals tend to relate the inability to orgasm to physiological factors. They believe that there is something physical that affects your ability to orgasm. The fact is that there are many more psychological and emotional factors that affect your ability to orgasm. That's why the exercises in this book have been presented so that you can put yourself in the proper frame of mind. When this occurs, you are able to truly make yourself feel open and liberated. When you find this sense of liberation, you can then go about enjoying yourself to the fullest. So, what's holding you back?

The fact is that there is any number of issues which can wreak havoc on your mind at any given point. In particular, being uncomfortable with your body can play a largely detrimental role in helping you liberate yourself. You see, we tend to compare ourselves to certain standards all the time. We compared ourselves to "good" mothers, "successful" professionals, or "good-looking" people.

When it comes to you, and your physical appearance, there is no need to compare yourself to anyone else. Sure, you might be keen on improving your physical conditioning and fitness. But that doesn't mean you are not attractive. If your partner values you for who you are, then you already have the most important aspect of attractiveness. This is why it's important to let go of such hang-ups in the bedroom. Being too overly focused on this aspect will limit your ability to truly enjoy yourself.

Also, stress plays a huge factor in holding you back. When stress gets the best of you, it can be nearly impossible to shut your mind off. If anything, you'll be faced with nagging voices in your head that won't leave you alone. You might be really enjoying yourself when you are suddenly hit with a flood of thoughts regarding any number of things. These thoughts can totally undermine your ability to truly enjoy yourself.

To combat this, the breathing and relaxation techniques we have presented are highly effective. In addition, making time for yourself and your partner means that you have the freedom to enjoy yourselves without being concerned with other things. Just being able to forget about your phone for a while is enough to get you feeling completely liberated from the world around you.

Another crucial factor is to address any issues that may be driving a wedge between you and your partner. Unfortunately, all couples have issues, especially if they have been together for a while. Often, unresolved issues fester beneath the surface. So, you don't really see them superficially. But below the surface, they are clearly affecting the way you interact with your partner. As such, if there is anything that is affecting your relationship, it's important to deal with it, get it out of the way, and move on. If you let it sit there, it will gnaw at you. This will become evident as you engage in tantric practices. You might start okay, but if such thoughts should hit you, you won't be able to recover. You'll have no choice to get over it or struggle with them throughout your tantric sessions.

Getting to the big "O."

There is a general misconception that it is hard to get to the big "O." The fact is that it's neither easy nor hard. It's just a question of knowing how to go about it. This implies that when you are committed to the experience you are living, you can find the pleasure you seek. Many times, it's just a matter of getting lost in the moment. This is why we have mentioned the need to live "in the now." When you manage to get everything out of the way, you can find the path to true pleasure and ecstasy.

Unfortunately, the big "O" seems like an elusive target. This occurs when you are completely focused on getting there without really taking in the entire experience. This puts unnecessary pressure on you. After all, why make orgasms the main attraction to sex when there are so many other things happening?

This is an important consideration as sex is filled with various situations and occurrences. You have intimacy, touch, sights, scents, and also your role in giving your partner pleasure. With all of those things happening all at once, there is no reason why you should become fixated on just one.

When you let go of your pursuit of the big "O," you will find that everything becomes much more enjoyable. You won't find yourself completely focused on getting there. Rather, you will enjoy the journey, so to speak. It's a means of enjoying the read even if you don't reach the final destination. Sure, it would be great if you did, but if you don't, it wouldn't be the end of the world.

Something else to consider is that tantra allows you to build up enough experience so that you can learn exactly what buttons to push and when to push them. The various exercises that we have presented throughout this book will enable you to find the right spots for you. This means that you won't have to guess. You'll know exactly where the road will take you. Ultimately, this is a comforting situation as you won't have to doubt or second-guess yourself.

The path to the big "O."

Here is a very simple exercise which you can do to get you to the big "O" every time.

First, think about the road you will be traveling on. This could be a massage, a massage followed by sex, or perhaps just a moment of intimacy with your partner. When you visualize what you are about to do with your partner, it builds anticipation. This anticipation plays a nice erotic game with you as you become expectant of what can happen. When you build up with anticipation, you naturally become aroused. Unless you're not feeling up to it, just the sheer anticipation of a sexual encounter is enough to get your curiosity moving.

Next, see with your eyes what your partner is doing. Take in the sights, sounds, and scents of what's going. This could be a massage, cuddling, or intercourse. It really doesn't matter. The idea is to take in everything that's happening.

Then, close your eyes and try to "see" it in your mind's eye. Try to visualize everything movement, touch, or thrust. In a manner of speaking, you are translating what your body feels to what your mind can see. If you wish, you can limit your visual capabilities. For example, a blindfold or sleeping mask can work quite well.

Since your mind is occupied trying to recreate a visual from what you are feeling, you are more concentrated on taking in the sensory experience rather than actually seeing the events unfold. As you render these images in your mind, you will find that the sensory experience builds up.

After, try your best to anticipate the next move. If you are in control, say in a cowgirl position, try to anticipate your next move. In a manner of speaking, you are planning what to do next as you go. When you do this, you are building up even more anticipation. As such, you are avoiding a mechanical motion by transforming in order to into a fluid movement.

Lastly, as you feel the pressure building up, don't try to chase the big "O." Instead, picture that energy coursing through your body. Imagine how that energy can race through every fiber of your body. When you feel it rushing toward you, don't try to catch it. Just let it come to you. If you try to pursue it, you'll end up disappointing yourself as you may not end up catching up to it. In fact, orgasms can be quite elusive once you are really close. However, when you don't make a point of trying to catch it, then you'll find that it will simply come to you. And when it does,

you'll know it's there. You'll be able to relish in the feeling that comes with experience full-on pleasure. In the end, you won't have anything to surpass the feeling that comes with finding yourself completely immersed in this kind of experience.
If that isn't enough for you, then don't worry. There is still more to come!

Chapter 14: Individual Ecstasy

Thus far, we have presented an extensive approach that can lead you, at your partner, to find pleasure and ecstasy. In a manner of speaking, this is about working in tandem to reach this goal. However, pleasure is an individual feeling that may, or may not, be easily achieved. It's important to take this into consideration as it's not always easy to find the bliss that you seek. If only it were as easy as turning on a faucet.

This is why experienced tantra practitioners are just as able to find pleasure themselves as they are able to help their partners find it. This becomes even more important when an experienced tantra practitioner finds a partner who is new to it. By virtue of their experience, they can help the newcomer find the heights of sexual pleasure.

In this chapter, we are going to take a look at how you can help your partner find pleasure and ecstasy, especially in those cases when it is hard for them to focus, enjoy themselves, and make the most of your experiences together.

Helping your partner find ecstasy

There are times when, for any number of reasons, your partner just isn't getting there. This could be due to something like being unable to forget about a stressful event, or perhaps having trouble reaching the big "O." This is where both of you need to keep in mind that the goal is not to find the biggest possible "O" or to last for four hours. The main idea here is to enjoy each other's company. This ought to be at the forefront of your mind all the time.

As such, you and your partner need to drop all of the expectations and focus on being together. That's all. All you need is to focus on the moment by savoring all of the emotions that come with enjoying the time you spend together. When you look at things from this perspective, you can't possibly go wrong.

Consider this situation:

Your partner's head is just not in it. They had a hard time at the office or perhaps some work-related problems. They are upset and can't seem to relax. Consequently, they just can't seem to enjoy themselves. Now, the worst thing you can do at this point is to assume that it's something related to you. In other words, take it personally.

Why would you?

Unless the issue is between the both of you, there is no reason why you should take it personally. Sadly, some folks think that they're partner isn't into it because they aren't attracted or don't like sex anymore.

This could not be further from the truth.

In this regard, it's important to take the pressure off as much as possible. In fact, there are times when you might have no choice but to just shut things down. You may end up simply cuddling. There may be times when all your partner needs is reassurance. Sure, this sounds easy, but it can be really tough when you have your motor firing on all cylinders. In that case, you can make a game of it. Perhaps your partner might find it relaxing to watch you taking care of business yourself.

The point here is to eliminate pressure. Tantric sex is not the type of practice you can master when on the clock. Relaxation and focus are essential to making it work. Otherwise, it would be nearly impossible for you to find the way to ultimate ecstasy. Please try to make sure that you have zero expectations when going into the bedroom.

How so?

If you enter the bedroom thinking, "I am going to have five orgasms today," then anything short of that will be a disappointment. If you change that attitude to "I am going to enjoy my time with my partner," then you are setting a different kind of expectation. You are focusing your mind on what truly matters, which is, enjoying the moment with your partner.

Relaxation is the key

Stress and anxiety are mojo killers. You don't need to be stressed out about anything in particular to kill the mood. The regular stress of day-to-day life is enough to bury arousal and pleasure. This is why relaxation is a fundamental tenet of tantra. You cannot expect to have a full-blown tantric experience if you are not relaxed and fully prepared to enjoy this experience.

Nevertheless, finding the ultimate relaxation isn't easy. In fact, it can be nearly impossible to settle down and find the right path toward peace and calm. Here is where you can see that tantra is not about sex. If you reduce your encounters to merely sex, then you are missing the point. Sex is the ultimate byproduct of the intimacy you have built with your partner. If you can't enjoy that, then you ought to reassess your priorities.

What to do if your partner just isn't into it?

At first, it might be really disappointing, especially if you are all fired up and they are not. This can be especially frustrating if you don't have much time to spend together. Yet, getting upset is the last thing you want to do. Instead, trying to foster an atmosphere of relaxation is key.

When you set the stage for your tantric encounters, you have any number of tools at your disposal. You can rely on a quick massage to help your partner calm down. Or, you can practice breathing in tandem. And then there's meditation. Often, just lying down together and guiding them through a visualization exercise can help lighten the mood.

Here is a quick visualization exercise that you can do with your partner:

First, lie in bed together. It's best that you don't cuddle or hold each other as you want your partner to settle down. But, if you feel inclined to do, then that's fine, too.

Then, sync your breathing. You can count out loud using the 1,2,3,4 technique. Take three shallow breaths and then one deep breath. As you exhale, try to picture the air leaving your lungs and floating off into space.

After, take your partner through a visual journey. You can describe anything you feel your partner will enjoy. If you want to describe an erotic situation, that could work great, as well. The point here is to help your partner calm down by using any means at your disposal.

If you happen to fall asleep, that's great, too. Just the fact that you fell asleep is signal enough that the experience was relaxing. Ultimately, being patient with your partner is paramount to achieving the level of intimacy and connection you seek. Plus, who knows when you might be the one who needs a helping hand. In that case, your partner's patience would certainly be most welcome.

Being supportive and understanding

Perhaps the most important thing you can do when things aren't going too well is to be supportive of your partner. After all, if you weren't feeling your best, you would expect your partner to be understanding and supportive, right?

This is the reason why you need to focus on helping your partner feel as comfortable as possible, especially when things aren't going smoothly. In fact, just being there can be enough to give your partner the reassurance they need to feel better.

In contrast, if you get upset and make a big deal out it, then you can be sure your tantric session will go down the drain.

Consider this situation:

The male partner is having trouble getting an erection. This situation can be a potential dealbreaker. That is true if your only purpose is to engage in penetrative intercourse.

But then again, what if you threw that out of the window?

What if you figure out other things to do?

This is where being supportive and understanding play a huge role. After all, the male partner is already under enough stress. So, removing the pressure and replacing it with understanding is the best way to make things work.

Now, let's consider a different scenario:

The female partner can't seem to focus. Things are going as planned, but she just can't seem to settle down enough to reach the big "O." It seems that no matter how much effort is put into, she just can't seem to get there. This can be common especially in situations of high emotional stress.

So, the male partner, rather than feeling disappointed that his partner wasn't able to get there, can turn things around and help her relax. For instance, slowing things down by cuddling, kissing, and touching can all help reduce stress. Of course, this isn't a full guarantee that everything will suddenly turn around. But just being supportive and understanding is enough to get the female partner in the best possible frame of mind.

Please keep in mind that one of the core tenets of tantra is to help your partner reach their pleasure. While it is true that you are not responsible for their feelings, it is important to consider the vital role you play. You can be the guide that leads them down the path they need to take. All you are doing is facilitating the way. You are, by no means, the one who is responsible for their pleasure. As we have stated numerous times, this is a journey in which we must all go through. But your support, understanding, and patience are all key to helping your partner get the emotional connection you both seek.

It's a two-way street

Indeed, tantric sex is a two-way street. It's important to bear this in mind as "traditional" sex isn't always a two-way street. In fact, traditional sex is generally about one of the partners enjoying themselves while the other may, or may not, get something out of it.

This is very common when male partners are inconsiderate of their female partner's pleasure. By the same token, this can occur when females put unnecessary pressure on their male partner. As such, the female gets the attention she seeks while the male is under stress to perform.

These situations all reflect cases in which mutual pleasure is not the main focus.

Think about that for a minute…

When you are convinced that the goal of sex is to simply enjoy yourselves, you'll find that getting to the big "O" is not nearly as hard as you might think. But then again, the big "O" isn't the only thing you can shoot for. Just being there for one another is the most important thing that you can do to foster the intimacy you seek.

Ultimately, it all boils down to knowing that tantric sex is about giving and receiving. You ought to be cognizant of how important it is to play on both sides of the ball. When you are perfectly aware that it is just as exciting and pleasure to give as it is to receive, then you will uncover the true nature of tantric sex. As a matter of fact, experienced tantric sex practitioners will tell you that there is an incredible rush that comes from seeing your partner reaching the heights of ecstasy because you led them there. The same can be said about the type of ecstasy you can achieve as a result of being with your partner. This type of satisfaction is unmatched.

Lastly, helping your partner find their ecstasy is not your responsibility. In fact, none of what happens in the bedroom is anyone's responsibility. This is what makes tantra so great; you are doing things because you want to, not because you have to. There is nothing that says that you have to help your partner reach the heights of ecstasy. Your role is to be the guide for your partner, especially when they are going through a rough time. When you are able to do that, the level of connection that is built cannot be questioned. This is the type of rock-solid intimacy that builds strong couples regardless of whether they are in a committed relationship or not.

Chapter 15: Couples Ecstasy

By now, you are fully prepared to take intimacy to the highest possible level. This means that you are now ready to make the best of your experiences by sharing in the sheer pleasure that comes with enjoying time with your partner. You now have the tools to make the most of your encounters. This means that all you need is to take the time to put the exercises into practice. That is why we have stated multiple times throughout this book that the most important thing is to focus on what you are experiencing at the moment, the "here" and the "now."
With that in mind, this chapter is about enjoying tantra as a couple. However, this chapter goes beyond what we have already discussed. We are going to see how you can enjoy ecstasy as a couple, particularly during sexual encounters. This means enjoying some "Os" while also enjoying the pleasure which you can derive from your partner's satisfaction.

Taking turns

A common misconception in the world of tantra is that true mastery of tantra implies that the couple orgasms at the same time. While this is certainly an amazing feeling, the fact is that it is quite difficult to accomplish as men and women have differing rhythms. Consequently, you might be building up unrealistic expectations when assuming that you must both orgasm at the same time.
When looking at tantric pleasure, there is nothing wrong with taking turns. In fact, taking turns can be a rather liberating experience.
How so?
By taking turns, you are essentially freeing yourself up to fully enjoy pleasure. This means that you don't necessarily have to focus on your partner. You can let yourself go freely. This will open up the road to mind-blowing orgasms.
Of course, there is no need to feel guilty. This is hardly selfish as you are not taking your partner for granted. All you are doing is going with it. Then, you can totally devote your focus on your

partner. This will allow them to experience the same kind of pleasure you have.

The opposite also works very well.

Perhaps you are inclined to pleasuring your partner first so that you can free yourself up for the big one. Ultimately, it doesn't really matter who goes first. The only thing that matters is that you are both on the same page. It could be that on one occasion, you hit the big "O" before your partner does. On another occasion, it could be that your partner gets there ahead of you. As such, it doesn't matter. What does matter is that you both take the time to make your encounters as pleasure able as possible.

There is one caveat to taking turns:

Please don't feel that you are entitled to receive or obligated to give. In this regard, taking advantage of your partner can be dangerous insofar as creating feelings of neglect. Your partner may feel that you are only taking advantage of them while they don't get their fair share. By the same token, if you feel that you are only giving and not getting your fair share, then try to avoid feeling resentful or even cheated.

The key here is to foster communication at all times. When you foster proper communication, you are giving yourself the opportunity to be on the same page all the time. This is especially important when something doesn't go right. Rather than blaming each other, you can figure out what didn't work right and seek to rectify it. Over time, you will get into such a groove that you won't have to think things through. You will know exactly what to do and when to do it.

Reaching the big "O" together

One of the most challenging things about tantra is reaching that big "O" in unison. While difficult, it is not impossible. All it requires is careful pacing and synchronicity. Some couple strive to achieve this ability. They feel that being able to reach that big "O" together, even after multiple "Os" before that, can truly foster the intimate tantric experience.

Now, if you don't reach that big "O" together, it doesn't mean that you didn't shoot through the roof. But by reaching the big "O" together, you can make the most of a unique experience that is quite uncommon among average couples.

Here is an exercise which you can do to help you reach that big "O" together.

First, it's important to recognize each other's rhythms and patterns. Generally speaking, one partner tends to reach the big "O" sooner than the other. This is regardless of whether it's the male or female partner. Although males generally tend to climax sooner than females. As you become aware of these individual patterns, you'll be able to recognize the pace for each partner.

Next, sync your breathing as much as possible. When the action gets hot and heavy, it can be hard to keep the same tempo. The partner that is getting closer to the climax will generally breathe a lot faster than the other. As such, the partner who is breathing slower must help the other to match the slower pace. This is helpful in controlling orgasm, particularly in men.

Then, as your breathing syncs, you can then match your movements accordingly. In particular, if you feel that you are losing control, slowing the pace of the game down is essential. As you match your movements, you can regain that flow thereby matching each other's arousal. As you feel the tension build up inside one another, you can increase the tempo as desired.

After, talk to each other. You can develop a code word to signal your partner where you lie. A color code is usually the easiest. For instance, "green" means things are going well but not quite at the climax. "Yellow" can be used to indicate you are close while "red" means you are getting ready to blast off. The goal here is for both of you to stay on the same color. That way, you can increase or decrease tempo as the color code demands.

Lastly, don't try to time the big "O." Most of the time, one will get there slightly before the other. In fact, many couples indicate that one's big "O" is triggered by the other's orgasm. In a manner of speaking, one's pleasure gets the other over the edge. What could be better than that?

After the grand finale

What do you do following the grand finale is just as important as everything else that happened prior to it. Lots of couples enjoy lying in place when engaging in intercourse. They purposely make a point of not pulling out as this helps foster that intimacy between them. This is a perfect time to continue breathing in sync while taking advantage of the opportunity for kissing and touching. Many times, the emotions are so intense that it takes a while to recover from it. As such, pulling out immediately after the big finale tends to be a mood killer.

Once you have decided to pull out, it's important to savor the moment. While you might hear a lot of experts say you need to cuddle, spoon, or remain physically close, the fact is that it's up to you. You can choose to cuddle or perhaps just lie together. Sometimes, emotions are so intense that you're practically speechless.

Some couples like to shower together afterward. This provides even more opportunity for intimacy. Others would rather just cuddle up and spend time together. Others still like to spend some time just talking. You might find that these are moments in which you have the most heartfelt talks with your partner. This is why "pillow talk" has become synonymous with pouring your heart out.

Ultimately, it doesn't really matter what you choose to do. The important thing is to savor the moment with your partner. The last thing that you want to do is get up, shower, and get dressed immediately following a powerful moment.

Sure, you might experience some unusual feelings. There are cases in which folks mention that emotions get all stirred up, especially if you are going through a tough time. This can happen. But that's when both partners need to be on the same page. Often, you don't have to say a word. Just taking a minute to live the moment is enough to truly nourish your soul.

One final consideration

For those who believe that tantra is a set of rules which you must follow to the letter, they could not be farther from the truth. The fact is that tantra is a discipline which has a set of guidelines that you are completely free to mold in your particular means and ways.

After all, humans are all different. There is no question about that. The core issue lies in the fact that you need to discover what works best for you. This is why tantra is best practiced with a partner whom you have a relationship with. And while it's true that we have stated the fact that you can have a tantric experience with someone you have recently met, the best results come from practicing tantra with a partner whom you have full confidence in.

When you have full confidence in your partner, you are psychologically free to explore everything there is to explore your sexuality. To sum things up, anything goes! Yes, really, anything goes. This is why you need to go about finding what really makes you and your partner tick.

If you are into BDSM, that's fine. You can have a full tantric experience within the domain of BDSM. There is nothing in the tantra philosophy that says you can't engage in BDSM and have the full tantric treatment.

If your idea of having a tantric experience is to go out to a club and then hit the sack, that's perfectly fine, too. The point here is to find that balance that will help you reach the mind-blowing heights that you wish to reach.

For couples with kids and an overall busy lifestyle, reconnecting through tantra is a must. Try your best to clear your schedule, make time for each other, and just forget about the world. You don't need to run off on vacation for two months. Even a single afternoon can do wonder for your relationship. By being able to let go of everything around you, you can find the peace you need to really get in touch with your sexuality. Best of all, this isn't the type of practice you need to spend money on. You can set the stage in a very simple manner, have the house to yourselves, and have at it.

Tantra is about finding the zone that will eventually lead you to that impressive feeling of lust, connection, intimacy, and pleasure. In the end, you don't need to have a complicated set of positions and rituals. With tantra, what works for you is what works best. Please resist the temptation to compare yourself to others. They do what works for them. You do what works for you. Ultimately, this is the goal of tantra. In the event that you have multiple partners, then you will realize that different approaches work for different couples. As a result, becoming familiar with the person you are with is the fundamental axiom of tantra.

Conclusion

Thank you very much for taking the time to read this book. We hope that you have found everything you wanted to know about tantra and how you can make it work for you and your partner.

Now, you might be asking yourself, "what's next?"

If you haven't already started trying out the exercises we have laid out in this volume, then the time has come to do so. If you feel your partner is on the fence, talk to them! Ask them to read this book, too. It could be that they just need a little more information about the topic.

Once you are ready to try things out, the most important thing to keep in mind is to go slow. Don't rush things. The biggest mistake that couples make when starting out it to rush things. Allow things to flow naturally. Eventually, you will find your own rhythm. By then, you will have the experience you seek to find.

Please keep in mind that anything goes with tantra. As long as you follow the main guidelines we have set forth in this book, you will find the overall tantric experience to be the most rewarding of your life.

So, what are you waiting for?

The time has come for you to savor the most amazing sexual experience of your life. You will find that once you go tantra, you won't go back.

Thank you once again for taking the time to read this book. If you have found it to be useful and informative, please tell others about it. We are sure they too, will find it useful.

See you next time!

Description

Are you looking for a tried and true way of enhancing your sex life without all the gimmicks and tricks you find on the internet?

Are you looking for a way to spice things up with your partner but don't really know how to mix things up?

Are you looking for a way to improve your understanding of sexuality but aren't into BDSM or anything kinky?

Are you looking for a means of improving your emotional connection with your partner that's both holistic and natural?

If you have been thinking about any of these questions, then this is the book for you.

In this volume, you will learn about tantric sex and how it can help you find the perfect balance between you and your partner. In fact, you'll be surprised to find that tantric sex has been around for a very long time. Yet, many of us are yet to discover it. But when you do discover it, the experience you are able to unleash is unlike anything else you may have felt before.

In this book, you will learn about the following:

- The fundamentals of tantric sex and what it involves
- The role meditation and relaxation in tantric sex
- Exercises which can help you sync your entire movements
- The ways in which tantric sex can help you discover new levels of pleasure
- How to pleasure your partner while pleasuring yourself at the same time
- How to engage in sexual activity without thinking about "sex."
- How to foster intimacy and build mutual trust

- Making the most of the time you have with your partner so experiences are truly memorable
- Recommended positions that will surely leave you wanting more
- Discovering the ways in which orgasms can lift you to new heights

… and so much more!

If you are expecting a book filled with sexual positions, then you will be surprised to find that tantra is so much more than that. You will discover how the right mindset is fundamental in ensuring that you find the greatest amount of pleasure.

Also, you won't find a collection of "tips" on how to improve your sex life. You will find a treatise on how you can turbocharge your sex life so that it's the best that you can make it out to be.

These aren't just bogus claims.

There are claims made based on experiences and years of practice and study. In anything, you get the best of both worlds: philosophy and practice.

So, if you are ready to make the huge leap from a traditional sex life into the tantric way of life, then you have come to the right place. Take the time to go through this book. You and partner(s) will never go back to the traditional sex way of life ever again!

Come on, then, let's get started discovering the art form that is tantra today!

Thank You

Thank you so much for reading my book.

I hope it opened your mind a little bit about Tantric Sex ☺

So THANK YOU for getting this book and for making it all the way to the end.

Before you go, I wanted to ask you for one small favor.

Could you please consider posting a review on platform?

Posting a review is the best and easiest way to support the work of independent authors like me.

Your feedback will help me to keep writing the kind of books that you like.

How to Talk Dirty:

Transform Your Sex Life & Spike Up Your Libido. 200 Real Dirty Talk Tips to Drive Your Partner Wild. Make Your Partner Your "Sex Slave"

© Copyright 2019 by CHASECHECK LTD - All rights reserved.

The content contained within this book may not be reproduced, duplicated or transmitted without direct written permission from the author or the publisher.

Under no circumstances will any blame or legal responsibility be held against the publisher, or author, for any damages, reparation, or monetary loss due to the information contained within this book. Either directly or indirectly.

Legal Notice:

This book is copyright protected. This book is only for personal use. You cannot amend, distribute, sell, use, quote or paraphrase any part, or the content within this book, without the consent of the author or publisher.

Disclaimer Notice:

Please note the information contained within this document is for educational and entertainment purposes only. All effort has been executed to present accurate, up to date, and reliable, complete information. No warranties of any kind are declared or implied. Readers acknowledge that the author is not engaging in the rendering of legal, financial,

medical or professional advice. The content within this book has been derived from various sources. Please consult a licensed professional before attempting any techniques outlined in this book.

By reading this document, the reader agrees that under no circumstances is the author responsible for any losses, direct or indirect, which are incurred as a result of the use of information contained within this document, including, but not limited to, — errors, omissions, or inaccuracies.

Table of Contents

Introduction
Chapter 1: Introducing Dirty Talk
    What Is Dirty Talk?
    Is It Inherently Disrespectful?
    Bringing Up the Idea of Dirty Talk
    Tips for Introducing Dirty Talk
Chapter 2: Dirty Talk as Foreplay
    Turning Your Partner on With Dirty Talk
    Better Sex With Dirty Talk
    Creating Sexual Tension With Dirty Talk
    Tips for Dirty Talk
Chapter 3: Dirty Talk for Men
    What Men Want to Hear
    Turning Men On
    Dirty Talk Foreplay With Men
    Dirty Talk During Sex With Men
    Steps to Dirty Talk With Men
    Phrases for Dirty Talk With Men
    Tips for Dirty Talk for Men
Chapter 4: Dirty Talk for Women
    The Right Approach
    Talk and Touch
    What She Wants to Hear
    Phrases for Dirty Talk With Women
    Dirty Talk During Foreplay
    Dirty Talk During Sex
    Tips for Dirty Talk for Women
Chapter 5: Digital Dirty Talk
    How to Sext
    Pacing for Good Digital Dirty Talk
    Overcoming Awkwardness of Digital Dirty Talk
    Taking the Perfect Picture
    What Not to Do during Sexting
    Tips for Digital Dirty Talk
Chapter 6: What NOT to Do
Chapter 7: Bonus Tips to Spice Up the Bedroom

Conclusion

Introduction

Dirty talk: It is something that too many people feel awkward about. So many people find that even talking about sex in a normal way is just too much. There are people that are embarrassed to talk about what they want or how they feel. They are embarrassed to use words to describe what they enjoy or what they dislike, and unfortunately, that embarrassment of talking about what is wanted is linked to a lack of intimacy as well.

What makes sex good? For some people, it is intimacy. For others, it is the raw, unadulterated passion. For others still, however, it is the simple act of communication. It is the communicating of what you want in bed; it is the idea that you can tell someone else precisely what it is that you want so that you can get it. If you want mind-blowing sex, then you need to know how to tell people what you want, and until you can do that, you will never have sex that is as good as you would like it to be.

There is an easy answer to being able to manage your sex life and make sure that you are getting that mind-blowing finale that you have been wanting. You can learn to make your partner want you more than ever just by learning how to communicate better in ways that are both erotic and informative at the same time. The answer is with dirty talk.

Dirty talk is talking about the acts that you would like to do with your partner in a way that is arousing. It does not need to be demeaning or violent—but it certainly can be if both partners are in agreement. For some, being called a slut in the context of dirty talk can be highly arousing—it can elevate the experience that is being had. For others, that is not okay. It is important for you to understand what it is that you can and cannot say to someone else to keep them hot and bothered, and this book will be your guide.

As you read, you are going to learn all about how you can introduce dirty talk into your bedroom. You will learn how you can drive your partner *wild* for you with just a few simple words and learning to understand what it is that they want to hear. We are going to be going through what dirty talk is and how it serves as a sort of foreplay for your relationship. We will go over dirty talk for both men and women, as well as a guide to sexting and digitally talking dirty to your partner. We will consider what *not* to do when you want to talk dirty, and we will finally look at some bonus tips that you can use to help spice up your bedroom with minimal effort. You will drive your partner crazy for you, and all you have to do is learn how to talk to him or her.

Remember, keep an open mind as you read. You are not trying to learn to say things that make your partner feel bad; you are saying things that will bring your partner pleasure and enjoyment. Yes, you may be saying things that are offensive in the moment if you and the other person were in any other situation, but oftentimes, in the moment when you are bent over, or have the other person bent over, it can be incredibly erotic to be called a name. It can be erotic to tell someone to suck your cock in the right context, or it can be horribly offensive.

Dirty talk does not come easily for everyone, and some times, it can be more difficult to use than people would expect, but you can usually work through it and become an expert at turning your partner on with just your words. You can use just those simple words to bring the other person to their knees, maybe even literally, just by knowing all the right things to say.

Keep in mind that this book is, by no means, supposed to make you an expert at sex, nor is it a medical guide to try to up your performance. It is here as a reference with all sorts of suggestions that will help you spice up your sex life and drive your partner crazy. Will all of these suggestions work on each and every individual person? Probably not—but they are worth a try.

Chapter 1: Introducing Dirty Talk

Imagine this. You're in the mood, but your partner is sitting across from you on the couch, reading a book, and not seeming interested in the least. What do you do? You could say, "Hey, get over here, let's bang," but let's be real here—is that going to work? For some people, maybe. Some people are totally happy to jump to it and get some without having to work up to anything. There are some that are always DTF. But, that is not always the case by any means. Telling your partner to get over here and fuck you is probably not always going to work, and even if that does work for you right off the bat, there is a chance that just a quick session of wham, bam, thank you ma'am (or sir), is not going to do it.

If your partner is not really in to just being summoned for sex, then doing so will not help you. If your partner is okay with that, you may find that you want to bring your sex life to the next level. Thankfully, you can do both quite simply—all by mastering the art of dirty talk. If you can use dirty talk the right way, you can turn your partner on so much easier than you would probably realize. It is not some crazy, magical act that can only be done in the bedroom either—you can use it to build up that sexual tension to drive your partner wild. All you have to do is know how to use it tactfully.

What Is Dirty Talk?

Dirty talk itself is not inherently dirty in any way. It does not have to be aggressive, violent, disrespectful, or anything else—it is literally just speaking about sex. It is basically just being willing to talk about erotically. Like sex, it is just as personal to the individual receiving it. Not every person is approached in the same way, and you need to be able to tailor what you are saying to the person. It can be offensive to one person or highly erotic to another, and may even vary based on the context

Of course, however, you still have to learn how to do it in the first place. Just as sex requires exploration and learning how to perform and how to create the best time for both you and your partner, you will have to experiment with your partner and talk about what you both like and what you don't, but eventually, you will have it down to an art. You will create the right kind of talk that will drive both of you insane, and you will love it. It supercharges the tension in the air and can really help to elevate the experience.

Dirty talk is surprisingly easy to use—in general; it is as simple as saying what you want and what you like. This essentially allows you to describe what you like at any point in time so that you can drive your partner wild. Men love to watch what they are doing. Women love to hear what is liked. This means that if your partner is a woman, they are already likely to be highly susceptible to the talk in the first place—they will love to hear what you are enjoying.

We will be addressing dirty talk for men and women later on in this book, but ultimately, women are going to take more work to build up to the fullest potential pleasure that they could enjoy. This means that if you want to heat things up quickly, dirty talk is your best bet.

Is It Inherently Disrespectful?

Of course, you may have your own reservations. If the idea of calling your partner crude names and demanding that they do lewd things to you is not your idea of a good time, or if your partner is not receptive to that, you can still talk dirty. There are no rules that say that your words have to be disrespectful or even particularly derogatory. Even saying things like, "Wow, you feel so good," or, "I love it when you move like that," constitutes dirty talk—and that kind of feedback can drive someone insane if you can do it just right.

Of course, it may be that in the moment, you and your partner genuinely do enjoy being more forceful or enjoy being able to call each other names. We all have different interests, and if you and your partner decide that you are into it, that is fine, too. There is nothing wrong with calling your partner a slut if your partner is receptive to it in the moment, and it serves to turn your partner on, and you both consent to it, it is fine. Just as with any other sexual act, all that matters is that both parties are willing.

Bringing Up the Idea of Dirty Talk

When it comes to bringing up the idea of dirty talk, you may be lost. It can be difficult to figure out where to begin, or even if your partner is going to be receptive in the first place. Not everyone is, but you can usually begin to figure out how to understand your partner with some experience. Think about your first time in bed with your partner. Was it great? For most people, first sexual experiences with a new partner rarely are as good as those that happen long after the fiery passion of the honeymoon period is gone, and why is that? Because you learn what turns each other on!

You learn exactly where all of those little physical buttons to press on your partner ar. You learn what he or she likes and what is disliked. You learn what is going to help them get the best orgasm that they can and what is going to ultimately lead to them not finishing at all, unsatisfied and annoyed. It's only natural— you won't know how someone else's body works until you have had the time to experiment with them. It is only then when you learn how their body works, or if you have very explicit instructions on what they like, that you can actually do what they want when they want it the first time.

You need to go through the same learning process with the mind as well. Some keywords may be enough to drive your partner wild, or some words may just be an immediate turn off depending upon their past experiences, and you will need to figure that out with time. If you can go through the struggle of learning what they like, you will be able to really enjoy each other. You can do this by talking about it. Dirty talk really is nothing but asking each other what you like and what you do not. It is talking about what you want to do and what you do not want to do. You can start off incredibly lightly at first, slowly working up to something a bit more intense when you have gotten good responses.

Light dirty talk

To begin with, you want to start with some basic talk. Imagine this; for example—you are at work and really wishing that you could get your hands all over your partner. You could text a quick message saying, "I miss you," or even with a winky emoji added to it or something else suggestive. Or, you could ramp it up a bit. Instead of something not particularly explicit, you would instead send them a message stating, "I miss the feeling of your tits in my hand," or something else similar. NSFW? Sure. But there is nothing particularly demeaning or even shocking in that particular message. You are telling your partner what it is that you miss and what you want. This is one of the unspoken rules of dirty talk; you have to be willing to tell them what you want in the moment so that you can get it, and because you are telling your partner that you want them, you are turning them on too.

Pay attention to how they respond to these light messages of what you want. It is important that you know what it is that your partner will be receptive to. Usually, early dirty talk is much more innocent, so to speak—it is talking about what you like and is usually more affectionate. It involves messages such as:
- I love the way you feel
- I need your body right now
- I'm so turned on by you right now
- I love your hands right there
- You look so sexy right now
- I love what you are doing right this moment
- You feel so good

You usually won't see many protests to most of this dirty talk; in fact, if you tell your partner that he or she is driving you wild, they will probably respond well to you. They will feel that tension building within them, and you will probably have a better time.

Moderate dirty talk

After enough light, dirty talk, it is time to consider some more moderate talk. This is usually a bit more explicit. You may find that at this stage, your partner gets even more excited in the moment, or you may find that you have reached that boundary point, especially if your partner voices that he or she feels taken advantage of, dirty, annoyed, or unhappy with any of this talk. However, if your partner responds well and seems to be turned on, even more, you know that you are on the right track. These are phrases such as:
- I want to dominate you/I want you to dominate me
- You have the perfect pussy/cock
- I love how you ride me
- Fuck me louder
- I'm going to pound you tonight
- I want you to pound me harder with your big dick/cock
- I love sucking your cock/licking your pussy so much

As you can see, at this level, you are getting a bit more explicit. You are starting to use words that, in ordinary circumstances, would be deemed vulgar or inappropriate. They can be offensive to some people, so you will need to make sure that you know where your partner draws that line.

X-rated dirty talk

Here, you are looking at dirty talk that usually is not going to be brought into a relationship that is still new. You are using this kind of talk for a partner that you know is going to be comfortable with it, and usually, you want to slowly build up to this, if your partner is receptive. This is overtly sexual; it is the kind of talk that is going to only be reserved for talking behind closed doors, or possibly through texts in private, but these are not phrases that would, under any means, be appropriate in any context beyond sex with someone.

- Show me how wet my slutty little pussy is
- Fuck me harder
- I want to be your little fuck toy
- I want to ruin your pussy
- I want you to ruin my pussy
- I want you to fuck me harder
- I want to taste myself on you

Some people are into this, but others would balk at such talk at any point in their relationship. It is important to recognize that everyone has their own boundaries that you will need to respect. Dirty talk, even when based in this kind of language, should still be adhering to the boundaries of your partner. Sex is intimate, even amongst strangers or during one night stands. It is a deeply personal act to give your body to someone else, and no matter the context, no matter if you are into BDSM, talking dirty, or anything else, the important part to emphasize is always consent and boundaries. Of course, you only know what those boundaries are if you can talk to the other person to figure out what theirs are in the first place. Communication is key.

Tips for Introducing Dirty Talk

So, you want to add dirty talk into your relationship. It could be great fun for you and your partner, and there is a good chance that you will find something that works for both of you. It may feel intimidating, but the best thing that you can do is get started. Start small and work up to what it is that you want to do. Make sure that you ask your partner during times that are not sexually charged about their own preferences and if anything stood out to them during your last romp.

If you are getting ready and don't know where to start to introduce dirty talk, then pay attention to these tips that are being provided for you. They are great starting points to begin talking about what it is that you and your partner want out of your relationship, how far you are both willing to go, and how you can both get the most potential enjoyment out of it. Try it and start slow—you will probably find that your sex gets even hotter than it ever was.

Talk about what you want

When it comes right down to it, you should make sure that you always talk about what it is that you want. When you are sending messages to your partner, or even just talking to him or her when you are not able to actually get down to business, you can drop little hints to drive the other person crazy. Tell your partner what you want. "I want you right now." "I wish I could feel your hands on me." "I miss the way that your breasts/hips/ass feels." Those are all starting points—you are telling your partner what you ideally want at that point in time, and that will drive them wild.

During sex, tell your partner what you like

During the actual act, make sure that you give feedback to your partner. Tell them what you like. Tell them what is really working for you. Make sure that you tell them what it is that you want if what they are doing is not quite doing it for you. Dirty talk is there to bridge that gap in communication. It is there to get comfortable with the idea of communicating about your own sexual desires and preferences without feeling ashamed or bothered by it, while simultaneously setting the stage for it.

Talk about it before the moment

Make sure that you have some time before you even begin to use it, where you and your partner have a genuine discussion of what you want out of your sex that you are having and what you like to hear or what you dislike hearing. Maybe there are some words that simply drive you insane, and not in a good way—before you begin to add dirty talk to your relationship is the best time to go over that. Make sure that you are communicating effectively.

Learn to be assertive

You have to be assertive in sex. Make sure that you are able to tell your partner exactly what you want or what you do not want. If they ask you if they can cum on your face, but you say that you are not into that, fair enough. You need to be able to say no, or say, "Hey, what you're doing really isn't for me. Let's forget about that." It is okay for you to say no about something that you do not care to do; in fact, you should say no to avoid resentment, which will destroy your relationship far quicker than anything else.

Don't be afraid to ask for something

Similarly, make sure that if there is something that you really want, you need to be willing to communicate about it. Don't hesitate to ask if something that you want is in your mind; you can always ask. Worst case scenario, you are told no, but really, that's better than feeling like you're denying yourself because you are too shy to ask.

Get creative

Make sure that you are using adjectives to describe what you are feeling. Think about the way that you want to describe your partner and see how he or she responds. Are they turned on when you tell them that they are beautiful/handsome, or do they respond better being called dirty or naughty? Everyone has different preferences, and the sooner that you can figure out what your partner's preferences are, the sooner you can begin to use them to entice them.

Don't forget your verbs

Yes, what you are doing is fucking—but use some other words in there too. Make a call to action. Talk about what you want and use verbs that will paint the picture of what you want. After all, "I want to make sweet love to you," has a totally different connotation than, "I want to fuck you so hard that you won't be able to walk tomorrow." Think about what it is that you prefer to talk about and also what appeals to your partner.

Compliment your partner in the moment

In the moment, make sure that you offer your partner compliments. What are they doing that drives you crazy? What makes you hotter? Do you like how they are moving or what they are doing? Compliment it? "God, your hair looks so damn sexy when you're on me," or "Wow, your touch feels so good." When you do this, you let your partner know that you are, in fact, enjoying every moment of what you are doing with them, and that will turn most people on more than anything else.

Narrate what you will do

Another great starting point is to narrate what you are about to do. Make sure that you, in the moment, let your partner know what you are about to do or what you are doing. "I'm gonna fuck you so hard right now," just before you start, or "Fuck, I'm gonna cum" or something along those lines. When you narrate like that, you put your partner in your mind as well. You are showing them the idea that you are enjoying what is happening. You are showing your partner how much you are having fun, and that matters in the moment.

Check in after sex

Dirty talk doesn't end when the fun does—you also need to talk to your partner after the fact. This is a sort of aftercare; it helps to show that your partner matters to you, and that will help to enhance what happened. You can talk to your partner about the actions that you enjoyed or tell your partner what they did so well, and you let them know that you continue to think about them and the fun that you had after the fact.

Take some of your dirty talk outside of the bedroom

When you are standing with your partner while doing something together, don't forget to add in your double entendres here and there to remind them that you are thinking about what you are doing. Even innocent comments can do the job for you. Imagine that your partner wears a deodorant that smells very distinct; perhaps it is a floral one. When you are at the grocery store talking about the candles and trying to choose one out, you can point out one that smells similarly and make a comment about it that lets your partner know that you are thinking about them, their scent, and the passionate fun you had in bed.

Experiment often

If you and your partner are still trying to figure out what it is that you want or like, you can, and should, experiment often. Bring new talk to the bedroom and mention it when you talk. Bring your desires to life all around you. Talk about what you want to do when you get the chance to do so.

Find inspiration

Sometimes, you will see some things that are highly erotic on television, or you'll read a book that has a particularly provocative line in it. Keep in mind that ultimately, television, books, and porn are just fiction—but the words used can still be deeply powerful and can be highly erotic as well. If you are having a hard time coming up with the right words to use, you can make sure that you do talk the right way to the person that you are around.

Get used to talking about sex in all sorts of contexts

A great way to help yourself figure out what you can do to eliminate some of the taboo is to start talking to your friends as well. No, you probably won't be telling your friends that you want to take them, bend them over, and fuck them, but if you can get used to saying so many of those words on your own even in normal conversations, you will be more able to talk to your partner as well. You need to be able to say words that you will need to use in the moment with them.

Expand your vocabulary

Another great starting point is to figure out the words that you are comfortable using. Make sure that you have a list of those that you won't mind making use of regularly. It could be that you are fine calling a penis a dick, but if calling a vagina a pussy or a cunt is a problem, figure out what you do want to call it. There is no right or wrong answer here for you; you can choose the one that is just right for you.

Keep it simple

You don't have to start off talking like you are in the middle of a porno—make sure that you are using words that you are comfortable with, and you can even keep it short. As you walk past your partner, whisper, "I can't wait to have you," for example—that could be enough to drive him or her insane. You don't have to do anything uniquely spectacular or creative or spout off a long ode to your partner's genitalia to constitute dirty talk. Even the occasional comment could be enough for you and your partner to get off better than before.

Channel your senses

When you are thinking of saying something, make sure that you use something that plays on the senses. Sex is intensely sensual, and you want to bring the senses into things as much as you can. "I can't wait for tonight." "I need to taste you." I want to feel you." I love how you smell." Try to hit all of the senses when you are getting started.

Start slowly

You don't have to just rush into things to have good dirty talk. In fact, some of the best, especially early on, involves slowly adding it in. Bring it up, little by little, and tell your partner what you like and what you want. You'll be surprised at the end results.

Be playful

There should not be anything innately hurtful; it should all be in good fun. If you want to enjoy your relationship with your partner, you want to make sure that ultimately, you are using your dirty talk to spice things up and make things more enjoyable. There is no reason to make yourself or your partner feel bad.

Give instructions

It can help to stop and tell your partner exactly what you want in the moment. Instead of asking for it, tell them what you want. This is a great way to really get them in the mood. A lot of people like it when their partner takes charge and tells them what to do; they are happy to comply. If you are interested in something, you should tell your partner what you want.

Try roleplaying

Some people find that the dirty talk, in general, is simpler if they are getting into the mood through roleplay instead. You can ask if you and your partner can try a small roleplay scenario and see if that gets the words flowing.

Try via text or messages if you feel too self-conscious

Now, it may just be that you cannot look at your partner with a straight face and say, "I want you to fuck me. Hard. Right now." Fine, fair enough. It can take time to work up to something like that. But, what you can do is begin to send some suggestive messages. Leave a note in your partner's lunch or in their car to find. Send a text when you know they won't get in trouble.

If something doesn't work, talk about it later

If you find that you have said something to your partner that immediately kills the mood, ask about it later. It might not be something that you can talk about in the moment, but you can usually check in with your partner after the fact. It is important that when you are in a sexual relationship, you are able to check in after the fact, and if you get the idea that you have made a mistake, make sure you ask about it later.

Figure out their sexual triggers

Figure out what it is that your partner really wants. Figure out the language that gets them rearing to go and make sure that you use them regularly. Most people have certain terms that they use, and you should figure those out. What do they say to you when they talk about sex? Do they call it sex? Fucking? Love-making? You want to adopt their language surrounding everything.

Let them know how turned on you are

You should always let your partner know when you want to use dirty talk, when, and how turned on you are. You can let them know what you are feeling, and that brings awareness to it. You are making them feel better because they feel like they can be more confident with you; they feel like fucking you is that much more fun because you are giving them that little ego boost.

One-word dirty talk

Sometimes, all you need is one word. You can say, "Yes," or "Harder," or "Deeper." When you add just one word, your partner knows that they are doing a good job; you weren't able to say a complete sentence, and they know that you are enjoying it. Master this, and don't be afraid to whisper it to them as you go.

Ask them what they want

Sometimes, you can make things sexier in the moment when you ask your partner what they want you to do. "How do you want me to finish you off?" or "How do you want to cum tonight?" are great in the heat of the moment, and you are letting your partner know that you will take care of him/her.

Use it when your partner least expects it

One thing that you can do to consistently get others off is to let them know that you want to do something when they least expect it. Send a quick message that says, "I want your pants off when I get home," or something similar, and you tell your partner that you are thinking about them.

Use it often

Make sure that you are willing to talk regularly about what you want. This is a great way to build up that tension all day long and get your partner's engines revving and juices flowing. If you want a good fuck, make them want it.

Do some research

You can learn all about what to say and find new lines pretty easily. You can find online erotica and read over that to get some inspiration. You can get all sorts of new phrases that can be used there, and your partner may even go crazy for them.

Chapter 2: Dirty Talk as Foreplay

Men may be able to go from 0 to ready to go to the bone zone in an instant, but that doesn't mean that they *should*. Why rush to the end? Foreplay is defined as sexual activity of any kind before the actual act of sexual intercourse. Some people prefer foreplay—a lot, and for a good reason. Foreplay is like the appetizer before the main course. It is there to help your partner, and you both enjoy sexual acts more. Your body is not primed to always enjoy sex—there are certain criteria that have to happen. Think about it—have you ever had sex when you were not ready, if you are a woman, or if you are a man, have you ever tried to slide in before your partner was ready? Or before you were yourself? You can't—or if you can, it is not pleasant.

Arousal happens during the foreplay stage. Your body, and your partner's, prepare for sex, and as a result, you and your partner both end up enjoying it that much more as a result. Men get harder. They find that they have more sensation during the act. Women get wetter, making everything that much more enjoyable as well. Blood flows down to the genitalia during arousal, and as a result, everything feels better.

Foreplay is so important—you need it if you want to have good sex. Can you have good sex if you and your partner both happen to be insanely horny at the same time without needing that setup? Sure—but that is the exception more than the rule. If you want good, passionate sex, do not forget the foreplay.

Foreplay doesn't have to be physical, and it doesn't have to happen immediately before you actually have sex. In fact, you can enjoy it all day long, tantalizingly teasing your partner so that you know their blood is rushing, and they are ready for that end of the night finale. It will probably become even more sensual when you have had all day long to drive your partner absolutely crazy with your talk and with your actions. All you have to do is know how to turn your partner on.

Turning Your Partner on With Dirty Talk

During arousal, all sorts of different things happen in the body. Your body literally prepares for the act of sex when it is aroused—it prepares the proper responses that your body will need. Your heart rate increases, along with blood pressure and pulse—this makes sense if blood is being redirected to the genitalia to help with sensation. Likewise, blood vessels will dilate in the genitals so that they can become engorged with blood. The penis swells up as a result, and on women, both the clitoris and labia do as well. For women, the breasts will also swell up, and nipples become erect, and the vagina becomes lubricated naturally.

All of this happens so that the body is ready to have and enjoy sex. It is only when you are actually aroused that sex is actually enjoyable in the first place, and if you are not, you may come to enjoy it in the moment, or you simply dislike it the entire time. Either can happen as a result of what is going on. But really, do you want to enjoy your time? Start with the foreplay. It will put you in the right mood as well. You will be able to build the emotional intimacy that all good sexual relationships need, and you will also be able to lower inhibitions during the foreplay. It is intoxicating and heady, and the more that you play around with each other, physically or verbally, the better your sex will go. Foreplay helps to release the necessary hormones that will lower cortisol—the stress hormone—in preparation for the bonding and affection felt during the act of sex.

Better Sex With Dirty Talk

Foreplay is important—there is no doubt about that. But, if you want to have better sex with dirty talk, you can make it happen. Dirty talk makes sex better just because of the way that it works. We want to be lusted after. We want to feel like we are wanted. We want to believe that our bodies drive our partners insane and that our partners want to get back with us as soon as possible. It's not just about going through the motions; it is about the fiery passion and pleasure. It is about taking someone else's body and making it your own. It is about enjoying yourself more intimately than possible in other ways. Sex is fun, but there is so much more to it than that. It is inherently programmed into us, and it is there to make us bond with our partners. It creates those feelings of euphoria and affection that we associate with our partners. Foreplay and dirty talk will both elevate sex from "meh" to being hot and better than ever before.

Dirty talk makes sex better—we know that for sure. We also know why it does that as well. Let's talk about the ways that dirty talk can create a better sex experience for both you and your partner before we continue on with looking at how to make it happen.

You can tell your partner what you like and dislike

Good sex, the kind that blows your mind, is all about communication—so why not make that communication fun and pleasant? Why not make that communication something enjoyable? Why not make sure that the communication does the work for you as well? You could tell your partner one day that the sex that you have is great when they do that one thing, or you could tell your partner in the moment, "Oh, god, I love it when you do that!" as it is happening. Telling your partner in the moment is going to leave them on fire; it will automatically stoke their inner fire. They know that what they are doing right in that moment is working for you, and that is enough for them.

You are able to connect better

Sex is also about connection. Even with one-night stands, you are still making a connection between yourself and the other person to some degree; you are able to tell your partner what it is that you want or need out of the encounter. Connection matters and dirty talk can help foster it.

You can reignite a lost flame

If you are living with your long-term partner, you may find that your infatuation, that highly passionate, desire-laden feeling is replaced with something that feels less. All too many people will mistake what happens to their feelings with them losing their love for the other person. However, it is normal for infatuation to disappear. However, you can spark that flame of passion again in the bedroom. Dirty talk can help you find those feelings of lust that you thought faded away with the infatuation. With a bit of dirty talk, you can add some variety to the relationship so that you are able to maintain that spark and enjoyment with each other.

It is versatile

Even if you and your partner are not together right at that moment for any reason, whether they have to work or they have traveled or anything else, you can send them pictures that remind them that they are the one for you and that you want them more than they probably realize. You are able to figure out what it will take for you and your partner to keep that spark alight, and you will be able to help create that allure; your partner will be caught up with you and probably spend all day long, thinking about getting back to your bed.

You'll boost your confidence

The act of talking to your partner and seeing the effect that it has on him, or her is a great boost in confidence. If you want to make sure that you are confident, you want to make sure that you can confirm that your partner is attracted to you, and a wonderful way to make that happen is through the way that you talk dirty to him or her. It will make you feel so much better about yourself when you realize that the simple act of talking to your partner is enough to drive him or her wild.

You'll also feel more attractive as a result as well. You'll feel like, in saying those words, you can take control, and you can get exactly what you want when you want it, and that is highly compelling and powerful.

It creates variety

If you can talk dirty to each other, you are able to make sure that your sex life never gets boring. You and your partner are able to figure out everything that you will need to do to maintain your passion for each other. You will be able to try new things and really and truly enjoy them as much as possible to really make sure that your spark never fades.

You can use dirty talk as a segue into talking about new positions, bringing toys into the relationship, and even starting to experiment with new objects. It can help you transition to speaking about, and therefore trying, any of those kinks that you may have had but been afraid to talk about. You will be able to tell your partner about those things that you have kept hidden, not knowing how to bring it up.

It makes you feel better about what you are doing in the moment

When you and your partner can talk to each other about intimate acts like sex, you know that you can talk about just about anything, including aspects of your life. You can alleviate the pressure that comes along with sex—you do not feel like your performance is under complete scrutiny in the moment because you and your partner are both talking about your actions with each other. Your partner is saying what he or she likes and that will give you that boost that you needed to know to help yourself figure out that you do not actually have to worry about the pressure aspect of what is happening. You aren't worrying about if you are doing things right because you can see that ultimately, your partner must be into it if they are dirty talking back.

It makes sex feel better

Sex is not designed to be quiet. Think about it—we groan and moan and grunt sometimes. It is not something that is meant to be prim and proper—it is us giving into our carnal, most feral desires that we have, and that means letting go of needing to be quiet. When you tell your partner how good things feel, you help make it feel even better. You make it real by acknowledging it, elevating it to the next level. This also helps you to create that higher sense of fulfillment that you are looking for as well.

Ultimately, sex is better with dirty talk. We love it—it lets us communicate what matters the most, and it helps us to feel more in tune with our desires. That is highly important to consider, and the sooner that we recognize that, the better. Give it a shot. Let your shame or embarrassment go and talk dirty to your partner. You'll be surprised by how different things can be with it.

Creating Sexual Tension with Dirty Talk

Sexual tension is highly powerful. We see it used in media all of the time because of the effect that it has—it's *hot*. It's so fun to see the ways that people respond to each other when they clearly want to have sex, but are afraid to or they can't, or there is some sort of boundary that cannot be crossed. It typically involves delaying or denying sex. The sex could cause problems, such as at work, or because there is a reason that it would otherwise have social impacts that are wanted to be avoided.

In relationships, however, sexual tension occurs when two people want to have sex and are flirting but can't actually perform for some reason. Maybe you and your partner are both at a big family event, and there is no way to comfortably give in without being caught. Maybe you and your partner are staying in someone else's home, or your children are around, or you're apart for work. No matter the reason, however, you can encourage sexual tension.

While sexual tension between two people that are not sexual partners may be awkward and uncomfortable, in a relationship or with partners, it can help you maintain that hot sex life that keeps both of you going crazy for each other. If you want to be able to build your own sexual tension, you need to know how to make it happen, and usually, it should be happening all day long.

The longer you can stoke that tension, the better it will feel when you release it. After all, what is orgasm other than a sudden release of built-up tension? You can build that tension up higher and higher all day long if you know how to get started. Dirty talk is one of the easiest ways to begin building that tension so that when you get home or when you and your partner are with each other again, you will not be able to keep your hands off of each other.

If you want to create tension, all you have to do is follow some simple ideas, and usually, dirty talk is the easiest way to do so, especially if you and your partner are apart from each other. Your ability to create that tension is going to make your partner completely and utterly addicted to you, and you will be able to guarantee that they will not be able to keep their hands away. If you want that, if you want to know that your partner will be vying to get that release from you any way possible, keep in mind the idea of creating sexual tension.

Start in the morning and keep it going all day

One thing that you need to do if you want to keep that tension going all day long is to start first thing in the morning. We all usually rush through the morning; it is hard to really have time for each other when we have places to go and maybe even kids to shuttle around. But, the morning is the perfect time to start that fire. You can create that spark, leaving the orgasm for later, allowing you to continually stoke the spark until your partner can't stand it any longer.

As you're getting ready to part in the morning, whisper a few dirty phrases to your partner, even if you don't have the time to sit down and make it happen. If you can remind each other of what you are doing and what you think, whispering those phrases of sweet passion to each other, you can get that flame stoked, and in no time, they will be begging for you as soon as you reunite.

Send texts throughout the day

When you have a thought about your partner during the day, let them know. Remind them that you are thinking about them. Tell yourself that you can't wait to get them in bed with you. If you miss them, tell them what you want to do. They will love the little boost in their ego first thing in the morning. You could even slip in a quick picture if you wanted to; they will probably love it.

Get creative with your timing

If you want that tension to build, make sure that you are getting creative. If you are in the theater, you can whisper a comment that will make them blush, and you will probably instantly turn them on. A well-placed hand on a thigh with the right look and the right phrase will build up that tension and make it impossible to forget it. You will be able to make sure that ultimately, they can't stop thinking about you, and that is exactly what you need. If you want to make sure that your partner craves you and will do whatever it is that you want them to, this is one way to drive them insane.

Whisper in their ear or in the crook of their neck

You want to make sure that your partner will be as turned on as possible, and that means that you will want to use all of their senses. Hovering right by their ear and whispering to them when you can to deliver that moment of what you want them to hear is the greatest way to really deliver that double whammy of physical closeness, whispering in an erogenous zone, and then also saying something that you know is going to turn them on.

Tips for Dirty Talk

Now, if you want to start delivering the best possible dirty talk that you can to your partner, it is time to get down to business through all sorts of different tips and tricks that you can use. If you really want to drive your partner insane, you need to be able to use the right words to make sure that they really want you. We are going to go over another 30 tips right now that will help you to bring your dirty talk to the next level during your relationship. You will be able to take your foreplay from average levels to those that are burning with desire that will make that moment of release that much sweeter when you are finally able to satisfy that desire that you have for your partner.

Make it authentic

When you are using dirty talk, make sure that what you say is authentic. If you are really thinking about fucking your partner's brains out, then say that—or if you are thinking about that quiet sensual night that you had the other night, tell them that, too. You should not be afraid of what it is that you are going to say to your partner. Make sure that you are paying attention to the way that your authenticity is being received as well.

Make sure it is mirroring your partner

Watch your partner—pay attention to if they seem to want to engage. If they engage after you have reached out and left a sexual line to grab, then go ahead and continue. If they seem not to be into it for some reason, pushing probably is going to do more harm than good. Make sure that if your partner is the first one to reach out, you reciprocate as well.

Ask simple questions

If you are asking questions at all to be erotic, make sure that the questions that you ask are those that are simple to answer—they should be yes or no questions. Your partner is not looking to be quizzed—rather, he or she probably wants to enjoy the moment and asking too many times how they like something is probably going to kill the moment. Instead of texting your partner saying,

"What do you want me to do tonight?" which would put them on the spot and may be difficult for them to answer, you can ask, "Do you want me to fuck you hard tonight?"

Build up to it gradually

If you are building up your foreplay, even for the day, don't just jump straight for the X-rated script that you are thinking about; instead, build up over time, all day long. Start out with a quick whisper of, "I can't wait to get my hands on you tonight," for example, as you are passing by each other to go to work or wherever you go in the morning. Even if it might feel like a good idea to share your passion by saying, "Goodbye, you dirty slut, I'll punish you accordingly when you get home," as you're walking out the door, if your partner isn't feeling it in the moment, you're probably going to do more harm than good. Start out innocently and build up all day long. It's not a race to incinerate everything; slow and steady is always best when you have a whole day of tantalizing messages to share.

Skip the eye contact at first if it is making you uncomfortable

Eye contact can be intense for people, especially if it is not something that they are usually comfortable with. However, you do not have to maintain eye contact for dirty talk. In fact, you can even have dirty talk occurring entirely over digital means without having to see each other in person at all if you wanted to. You can talk to them separately if you wanted to. You don't even have to look at the other person if it is making you nervous. If you find that you lack the confidence that you will need to get to the sexy point that you want to make, find a way to skip out on the eye contact. You can build up to that over time.

Make a promise for later, and follow through with it

If you tell your partner that you plan on bending them over and thrusting with reckless abandon that night during your constant foreplay for the day, you will want to follow through with it.

Make that anticipation and reward it later on. Make sure that you always follow through with what you say that you are going to do so that you can make sure that ultimately when you tell your partner something, they know that you will follow through with it.

Inside jokes

Now, jokes may seem like the least sexy thing ever, but think of it this way—when you have inside jokes that are about your sex life, just mentioning the inside joke, or referencing it, can be enough to get your partner going with just a glance and a passing comment and no one else around you will be any wiser to what has just occurred. This is a fantastic way to approach the situation if you are trying to figure out how best to interact in ways that are not overt.

Say something with a double entendre

Imagine that you are eating a popsicle, sensuously sucking on it while making fuck-me eyes at your partner, smirking and saying that, "It tastes so good," or "Mmm…" as you do it. This is going to get your partner desperate for you without ever saying anything that is not really appropriate. The tone is what matters here, and the double entendre is probably enough to help your partner really feel like you want them. This is perfect. You could even lean over and mention something about wishing that you had them in your mouth instead.

Say something subtly possessive

Now, too much possessiveness and jealousy is obviously a problem in a relationship, but if you can play it off the right way and whisper it to your partner as you do, smirking, or flirting with them, you can drive them crazy. We innately like the idea of our partners claiming us as their own, especially when we know that it is not something that is meant from a bad place. It can be kind of sexy to hear our partners stake their claims over us, after all, especially if it is something like, "I want to make you mine."

It's all about the tone

Keep in mind that the tone of what you say is everything. If you want to drive your partner crazy, you have to use the right tone of voice, or you are going to find that he or she is probably going to lose interest. Think about it: would it be sexy for someone to tell you in a flat voice, "I love your cock/pussy."? No enthusiasm. No actual sense of enjoyment in there. Just a flat, robotic, "I love it." Would you believe it? Probably not. Would it stoke that fire within you? Probably not.

You need to master the sexy tone to master the art of foreplay, and that means making sure that your tone is something that you know they will find attractive. Go for something lower, throatier, and softer. Learn the voice. It's your sexy voice. Use it.

Read erotica to each other

If you and your partner are still struggling with being able to talk to each other honestly and from that point of sexual tension, then stop, take some time, and read some erotica that you can read back and forth to each other. This lets you get a feel for the writing and the phrasing. You start to adjust to saying the words in your mouth, and as a result, you get closer to stepping into the zone of being able to use your own dirty talk.

Be bold and take a chance

You never know how your partner will take what you are saying. Try taking some chances and saying some things that ordinarily, you wouldn't say, but that you decided to try out. Be bold. Say things that you think are hot, but that you wouldn't dare to say to your partner normally and see how he or she responds to it. You may be pleasantly surprised.

Make a game out of it

It could be fun to make a game out of trying to make each other blush. The point is to ramp up your sex talk until one of you or the other is blushing. Then, the other person is the winner in the situation. It can be fun trying to think of the sexiest, most blush-worthy comment that you can come up with in hopes of seeing what happens next.

Don't be ashamed as you talk

Don't worry about what you are saying; you are talking with someone that you have had sex with—you don't get much more vulnerable than having someone else's body part in you, or in putting your body part inside of someone else. Allow yourself to really come to terms with the sexual content that you are saying and don't mind it. You're saying things that are typically "inappropriate," but you have a very specific purpose for doing so—you are trying to turn on your partner. Let's face it—the act of sex itself, to someone who is not turned on, may seem a bit strange. It is messy and sweaty, and isn't it a little bit strange how we put our private bits together, and they somehow fit? Sex is strange. Nature is strange. The worlds that you use to try to turn someone on are probably going to seem strange too—but they serve a purpose. Let go of the shame and just do it.

Ask some dirty questions

Sometimes, it can help to ask questions that are dirty. "What do you think I'm wearing? How would you feel if I answered the door and was naked? What should I wear today for you?" Ask questions that start to hint on suggestive but are not all the way there yet. It starts to set the field for what you want to do—which is turn on your partner, and the sooner that you can do that, the sooner that you can get into bed.

Share your fantasies

If you have been dreaming or fantasizing about your partner, now is the time to share it. Talk to your partner about the dreams that you have been having or about what you want to do with your partner more than anything and don't hold back about it—the fantasies should be erotic, and you may find that your partner will even agree to do what you want to do without complaint. You may even find that you both share the same common fantasy!

Ask if your partner wants to take charge

If you want your partner to love fucking you, then you want to ask them if they want to be in control. Even if you are usually the one that takes the lead, ask them what they want. Figure out if they do want to be in the lead, and if they do, let it happen. You may find that you are pleasantly surprised by what happens next.

Tell your partner what you want them to do

If your partner is at home and you are at work, you can send them some sexy texts telling them what you want them to do right at that moment. Make it erotic, but make sure that they don't quite finish up the job without you. Let them know that you want to save the best part for you at home and that you're thinking about them doing it. This builds up that tension for you, and for them, you are both going to be dying to get into each other's arms.

Ask them to play dirty truth or dare

Again, if you want to create foreplay with dirty talk, games can be a great tool to use. You can set up, so you and your partner both play together and see where things take you. If all of the topics are erotic, you will both probably find that pretty soon, you're both desperate for the other's touch, and that means that your job was very well done.

Message them when you're masturbating

If you're going solo for a session and are apart, consider sending some sexy messages letting them know that you're thinking about them—*really* thinking about them. They will probably go crazy for it, and you can find yourself loving every single moment of it. You will be able to tease them with messages such as, "Oh, it's too bad you're not here, I could use some help ;)" or something similar to that to let them know that even when you're on your own, and even with the entirety of the internet's near-infinite and ever-expanding collection of porn, you chose to think about your partner.

Sexy riddles

You can use sexual riddles that are fun, but still erotic and send them or whisper them to your partner all day long, really building up that foreplay before your grand finale. Riddles can be something silly like, "What's hot and [skin color] and all wrapped up, waiting for you?" or something more erotic as well. Be creative. Be silly about it, but most of all, be erotic and sensual.

Tell them what turns you on

Make sure that you let your partner know exactly what it is that you want to do. Tell them what turns you on more than anything else, and they will probably use that to their advantage later on. Even better, if you are sharing turn ons, just thinking about them will probably get some juices or blood flowing, if you catch my drift.

Tell them what they do to you

If your partner is driving you crazy, let them know. Tell them just how passionate you are for them and just how much knowing that you can't be inside of them, or have them inside of you, right that moment is driving you mad. If you can do this, telling them just how passionate you are, you can boost their egos while also setting up that sexual tension for later on as well.

Tell them what you intend to do when you see each other next/the next time you are in bed

Let them know exactly what you're going to do next—tell them, for example, that you're going to tease them all day long, or that you're going to suck them or lick them or fuck them, or anything else that you're interested in doing. It will get them going crazy for you as well, and you will be able to see just how strong of an effect that you have on your partner when you do it. This is highly erotic and something that many people love to hear as well.

Create a template

If you struggle with dirty talk, it can help to have a sort of template, where you simply follow the lead and fill in the blanks to make it work for you. You could, for example, use some talk about what you love when they do something. Try this format: I love [action] when you [describe the action]. This can help you to begin to get that process down so that you can properly voice your approval or what really matters the most to you when you're getting down to business.

Create IOUs

You can create little sexual IOUs for each other as well. You can whisper to your partner what you want them to do to you that night, as well as whisper to them your promises for what you will do for them when you are able to get down and dirty that evening. The idea here is to create that anticipation for the night—it should be enticing and should drive you both wild. Hearing what you are going to do to each other is a great way for that tension that you need during foreplay to really be built up.

Ask them what they do when they are masturbating

You can also ask your partner what they think about when they are flying solo as well. You can use this information, hearing about what they do with each other so that you can begin to use that when you do have sex. This is a great way to open up conversations and connections about what you both like as well. It is a wonderful influence if you need to make sure that you are both able to talk to each other openly, and even better, it can turn you both on—you get to fantasize about your partner touching him/herself, and your partner gets the added benefit of thinking about you doing what they do.

Let them know about your favorite body part they have

Think about your partner and what attracts you the most to them physically—then compliment them for that body part. Let them know that their stomach or their abs or their breasts drive you insane and tell them all about how much you think about those body parts and what they mean to you. When you do this regularly, you are not only boosting confidence for them; you are also letting them know that you care about them and that you are paying attention to what they look like and how you see them. This is crucial; if you want to have mind-blowing sex, they have to feel confident enough to believe that you are attracted to them.

Talk about your own anticipation

Tell them what you can hardly wait for. Let them know that you are anticipating them. The idea that they are being lusted over is going to be highly erotic for them, and they will likely respond incredibly positively to it, meaning that you'll be able to have all the fun in the world when you can get together. Comments like, "I can't wait to feel you," or "I'm picturing us together naked right now, and I can't wait until we're alone so we can be," are great at stoking those flames and igniting that passion you want.

Chapter 3: Dirty Talk for Men

So. You want to get down with a man, do you? Do you want to make him hard with just a few whispers or a few words typed into your phone? You can make that happen—all you have to do is know what to say, and you'll get his blood pumping in no time at all. As you read through this chapter, you are going to learn all about what it is that will turn on a man with next to no effort at all—all you have to do is be smart about the way that you choose to communicate with him.

Dirty talk can be especially difficult to muster for many women who may feel awkward about what they will be saying. If you're a woman, or even a shy man, hoping to get it on with the man of your dreams, you need to learn one thing: Confidence is sexy. Take control. Take command of the conversation. Make sure that when you talk to him, you are brave about it and that you are willing to go for it. Many men are sex-driven—it is just part of their hardwiring. They are born to fuck, and if they can't, they feel defeated. They may feel emasculated if it is not clear from what you are doing or how you sound that you are enjoying yourself. They want to know what you think of them, especially during sex itself, and they want to hear what you want them to do to you as well.

Whether it is a well-placed moan, a few whispered words of affirmation that he is, in fact, getting you off, or even screaming his name with abandon, head thrown back in sheer ecstasy as you ride him, you have options and dirty talk for men is absolutely not a one size fits all sort of thing. However, one thing is consistent. No matter what, men want to feel validated in knowing that you are satisfied with their sex, either in the moment, leading up to the moment, or even after the fact. All you have to do is figure out how to tell him that.

What Men Want to Hear

Men, when in bed, are simple creatures. They want to know that you are enjoying them, and they want to feel like they are getting you off. If you can give them that, you are already going to escalate the sex to fantastic levels that your partner will most likely thrive on. Think about it—how validating and how much of a turn on is it for you if you are told that your sex is the best, or if you can see that the other person is loving every moment with you?

When you are talking to your partner, then your dirty talk simply has to inform him of one thing: That you want him to fuck you because you think that sex with him is fantastic. If your dirty talk conveys that, you are probably on the right track just like that. How can you do that, then? Simple—you can tell him what you want to do, or you can make use of moans when making out or riding him. You can tell him that he is fucking you so good or that you love it. There are so many options there—you just have to let him know that you are there, present and in the moment and that you would rather be there than anywhere else.

Turning Men On

When it comes to turning your man on, you have no shortage of ways. You could simply take off your own clothes, and he will probably be hard just thinking about the time that he can have with you. You can kiss him or touch him or tell him to fuck you there, or you could do it the long way, building up that sexual tension and making it so that he can't think about anything else. Turning men on is more than just touching some cock and balls or shaking an ass. There are ways to do so without ever laying a finger on him, in fact, and some of those can be even sexier than what you may do to him in bed.

Remember that ultimately, every man is going to be different. Every man is going to have his own preferences that you will need to consider, but if you are able to consider them effectively, you can also usually make it happen in very similar ways through seduction. If you want to turn your man on, consider these options to get that blood pumping and get him ready to go.

Smile seductively

The seductive smile is a great way to get him going, especially if you have just said something that could fall into a double entendre zone. Giving him a quick, sexy smile, especially if you let your eyes undress him within his attention, can drive him wild. You can do this across a room from each other, or you can do it in the middle of a conversation. Make sure that you have an intense gaze as you look at him and try to entice him over.

Be confident

Confidence is sexy, whether you are a man or a woman. If you can speak with confidence, act with confidence, smile with confidence, and more, you will find that he absolutely loves the way that you engage with him. Make sure that, no matter what it is that you are saying to him, you do it with confidence. Even if you tell him something that sounds borderline ridiculous when you first say it, if you can pull it off, you will find that he will go crazy for you in an instant. All you have to do is have that confident attitude.

Compliment him

Men *love* to be complimented. It gives him that ego boost that will help to turn him on even more, and it also shows that you are paying attention to him, meaning that you are getting him ready with two different tactics at once. If you want to make sure that you can get him happy, hot, and in bed, you want to give him the best compliments that you can think of. Tell him how smart he is when he helps you. Let him know that you think he's sexy when he's doing something. When you're in bed together, tell him how you are enjoying it. All of this will help you to turn him on with ease, and the sooner that you turn him on, the sooner that you will find that he will want to stick by you.

Dress sexy

Of course, men also love their eye candy. If you want him to think that you look great, then you have to act the part as well. Make sure that you wear something that you know that he would love. If he is into tight, black dresses, try wearing one. If he is into something else, try wearing that for him. He will greatly appreciate the help and will probably not hesitate to look you over.

Show some skin

Similarly, spending some time showing skin can help a lot as well. Wear shorts, short skirts, or short dresses, and make sure that they are low-cut. In particular, men tend to go crazy for the breasts, thighs, ass, neck, and back. Those are some of the most common parts that can turn a man on almost immediately, especially if he already likes you. You just have to play your part and let him enjoy the moment.

Hold eye contact

Eye contact is sexy. It tells the other person that at that moment, they are the only person on your mind, and that is enough to turn them on, man or woman. When you are able to connect with someone else through maintained eye contact and making sure that he sees that you are interested, you will turn him on.

Whisper what you want with him

When it comes to getting him hard for you, you can tell him exactly what it is that you want. Whisper in his ear that you want to ride him, or that you want his cock in your mouth. If you can tell him what you want to do with him, you will be filling him up with all sorts of anticipation and sexual tension, and he will not be able to get enough of you. You will drive him wild, all through dirty talk.

Dirty Talk Foreplay with Men

Foreplay is great for men and women—it can be incredibly fulfilling to have someone all over your body or even just in your mind. Foreplay, however, does not have to be only physical. You can tease with your voice, with your words, and even over text if you want to. You just have to know what you are doing and let it happen.

If you want to engage in foreplay with your partner, start with your words. Make sure that you tell your partner what you want to do. Don't overthink things—just say what comes to mind. What do you want him to do to you? What do you want to do to him? What are you thinking about right that moment as you are watching and wanting him? Think about those things and then verbalize them. The foreplay follows. As you tell him what it is that you want, you are usually able to ensure that your partner gets turned on quicker and that they are anticipating the sex more so that it is also more enjoyable as a direct result.

You can also talk to him about your secret fantasies—tell him what you're really thinking about and what you really want to try doing, even if you are afraid that he might laugh. Remember, confidence is sexy, and if you want to be confident, the best way to do so is to know what you are saying and how to drive him wild. The more that you drag foreplay out, the more eager he will be to finally get his hands on you for the big event, and you will notice a world of difference.

Dirty Talk During Sex with Men

During sex, dirty talk is easy. Tell him what you like. Tell him what you want him to do. Be as vulgar as you want. There are, of course, some considerations to make. Does he like being called "daddy," or would he prefer that you use his name? Tell him when you are getting close to finishing up and tell him when you are really enjoying yourself. The more that you can communicate how you are doing in the moment, the more turned on he will be as a direct result. If you want him to fuck you, tell him that. If you want him to go quicker or slower, tell him that as well.

Some men may prefer to be the ones in charge, but most of the time, they can respect being told what to do and how to do it. It can be sexy to be commanded about in bed, and men love that. If you really want to turn him on, and you want to do it well, you will be explicitly clear about what you want.

One thing to consider, however, is that you shouldn't try to censor yourself. Keep it vulgar. Keep it derogatory. Tell him that you want his cock inside of you, not that you want his genitals within your own. You want to make sure that it doesn't get awkward and going from sexy small talk to suddenly using anatomically correct terms can be a bit of a mood killer.

Steps to Dirty Talk with Men

Dirty talking with men doesn't actually have to be as intimidating as you may think that it will be. You can follow a few simple steps and figure out how to start talking to your own partner, no pressure involved. All you have to do is know what it is that you want to say, how you will say it, and how to keep it calm and natural. If you can do that, you will find that everything else is simple. You just have to work hard to give your partner that basic level of attention that will help him to feel like he is wanted, and he will be ready to go.

Start Small

Of course, you should always start small. When it comes to dirty talk, it can take a bit of time to get into that learning curve. For some, it is nearly instantaneous, but for others, it is highly difficult to get into the swing of things right away. You need to get to know each other, especially if you are in a new relationship. You need to know that your partner is actually interested in what you are saying or wanting and that your partner is open and receptive to what you are saying. If you can do that, you will find that everything else will follow simply.

Begin in privacy

Likewise, it is usually wise to start in private with your partner rather than being bold enough to get on with it in public. Some people may love whispering those naughty little words into each other's ears, but don't do that without first letting your partner know that they should expect you to do just that by doing it in private before ever attempting it anywhere else. This gives you the chance to make sure that you're both on the same page.

Personalize it

When it comes time to begin, make sure that your dirty talk is personalized. Don't just use random sayings and phrases that are not really tailored to anything. If your partner does not enjoy being called daddy, for example, calling him daddy constantly would be a major problem. Rather than doing that, it is more important for you to figure out what he likes. Does he like being told how good he feels? Does he like being told that he's doing a good job? Does he want you to beg for him to do something or to tell him what you want? Figure out what works for him—you'll know when he seems to get even more eager to fuck than before.

Keep it natural

Finally, don't overthink things. Let things happen naturally and say what comes to mind rather than attempting to come up with the cleverest thing that you can think to say. Rather, you should take the time to just say what comes to mind and see how he responds. It's trial and error, and really, is it that embarrassing to say something to someone that you are sexually intimate with?

Phrases for Dirty Talk with Men

- What do you want me to do?
- How do you want me?
- Your lips feel so good.
- Your [body part here is/are] so sexy
- I want you now.
- I want you to touch me here [guide his hand].
- I want you to fill me up right now.

- Cum in me.
- Fuck me harder.
- I want to do [name what you want] to you.
- I love your kisses.
- Your cock feels so good.

Tips for Dirty Talk for Men

Talk about it before you actually do the deed

This makes it so that you are both currently aroused and therefore are more likely to actually get somewhere with the conversation. Ask about what he wants to hear you say or how far he wants you to go.

Enjoy it in the heat of the moment

Spend time engaging in it whenever you can, and don't be ashamed when it comes to taking the time to enjoy it yourself. It is just as much for you as it is for him; make sure that you are paying attention to what is happening and how much fun you are having.

Pay attention to his reactions

Make sure that in the moment, when you are using dirty talk, you pay attention to what it is that his body language says. Many people do not want to admit when someone has crossed a boundary, especially during sex, but that is more important than ever to stop and point out the problem. If it looks like your partner is uncomfortable with an exchange, remember that.

Check in after the fact

When you are done with the sex itself, it is time for you to spend some time actually talking about what he thought. The act of checking in might serve as extra dirty talk and may turn him on even more. While they don't typically admit it, men are just as emotional as other people.

Take it outside of the bedroom

Your man will probably love a message every now and then telling him just how hot you're getting thinking about what he did the night prior or how much you enjoyed it in the moment. Take that time and capitalize on it.

Don't get discouraged

There is a good chance that sometimes, you will mess it up. Sometimes, you need to practice. It might be awkward at first. It might feel weird to say these things out loud, but it is so important to remember to remain persistent and to keep on trying. If you can have sex with this person, they probably won't judge you for saying something that misses the mark.

Reach out and tell him your current fantasy

Whether you are together or apart, you can tell your partner what it is that you are fantasizing about at that moment. Are you thinking about how much you want his mouth on yours or how much you want to feel his dick in you? Tell him that.

Narrate your enjoyment for him

When you are fucking, men want to hear your interpretation of what is going on. Let him know all about what it is that you are enjoying in the moment.

Invite him somewhere

Especially if you are at an event or something, you can whisper to him that you are going to go into an isolated area and waiting for him. This is a major turn on for most men, and he will love it.

Say things that are meant to be tempting

At random, you can drop something that you know will drive him crazy. Tell him that you're not wearing any underwear or that you've been peeling particularly turned on at that moment. Tell him all about that new wax that you got, or that you have something new in an intimate area that you want to show him.

Mind the voice

If you are talking to him, make sure that you use the best, breathiest voice that you can manage to entice him. Men love that breathy, quiet voice.

Tell him what you appreciate

Tell your man all about what he did last time that was entirely unbelievable to him. When you do this, you will not only turn him on when he realizes that something that he was doing was that great to you, he will also then be thinking all about what he did—further turning him on.

Wake him up with a sexy promise

You can also start by waking your man up in the morning and telling him all about what you will do to him that day at some point. Tell him all about what it is that you want to do to him so that you will be able to drive him wild. You could tell him that you had a sexy dream about him that you're going to reenact that night, for example, as you run your hand up and down his thigh, or you can tell him that you're going to blow him or fuck him or do something else that drives him insane.

Tell him when you're cumming

In the moment, tell him that you're getting close, and as you do finish up, let him know that you are. As annoying as it can seem in porn to some men, they actually find that hearing that they are bringing their partner to orgasm is actually incredibly sexy. So many people say that they are turned on knowing that their partner is turned on, and that is highly impressive for them.

Beg him not to stop in the moment

When you are having sex, make sure that when they are getting the angle or spot just right that you tell him that he is. Tell him how much he is driving you insane and let yourself enjoy it as well. It can seem weird at first to tell someone that you like it right there or like that, but men love the encouragement.

Tell him that you want to do that again

There is nothing more flattering than telling your partner that you want to do exactly that all over again. After all, most people won't bother trying to repeat their sex with people if it is not worth every single moment of it.

Ask for exactly what it is that you want in the moment

You can beg for him to do something else, or you can ask him to, and he will know that you are enjoying yourself and the moment enough to want to keep going and ask for what you want.

Or demand what you want

You can also demand exactly what you want from him as well. Some men are turned on by a take-charge partner, even when they are traditionally dominant, and he may respond well to you telling him that you want him to take you from behind, or to ride him or anything else.

Tell him to take you

When you give him your best fuck me eyes and tell him that you are his for the taking, he is going to be turned on almost immediately. It is sexy to tell someone that you want to be completely taken by them. It is almost like a gift, so to speak, with you offering up your body completely to someone else.

Ask to be used

Sometimes, the best sex is that which is completely without regard to standard expectations. You may not want to be used in your relationship, but there can be something about surrendering in the moment, and men can enjoy that.

Be yourself

Unless you've agreed to roleplay or something else, make sure that, at the heart of your dirty talk, you are still yourself. Don't say things that you don't actually want to say just for him. It is important that you are not forcing things and that you are following your own style. While you may never want to tell your partner to fuck your brains out and choke you (which some people may want), you might find that complimenting him as he fucks you to be your style, and that's okay too. Make it authentic and be yourself.

Ask if you can do something sexy

Sometimes just stopping and asking him for permission to do something for him can be a bigger turn on than just doing it yourself without waiting to hear if he wants to.

Tell him that you can't think about anything but his cock

Men love to know that you have them and their fucking, on the mind, and if you can tell him that all that matters to you in that moment is thinking about fucking them, you will turn them on in an instant.

Tell him that you're touching yourself while thinking about him

What is sexier than knowing that your partner is fantasizing about you while touching themselves? He will love to hear this.

Tell him to cum for you, or even in you

Make sure that you tell him that you want him to cum for you when you are ready, or you could even offer to let him cum in you. Men love being told that, and it can instantly escalate the situation.

Tell him to look at you

Eye contact can absolutely escalate the situation and make your partner go crazy for you, especially during the most intense moments.

Say his name

Men love to hear their names said out loud to them. Yelling, whispering, moaning, it all depends upon the individual man, but they generally love to hear it said. Just make sure that you don't accidentally use the wrong name.

Tell him how good the sex is

Men want to be validated, and you can do that by telling him just how well he's doing. Men love to hear all about how satisfied they are making you, and if you tell him just how much you're enjoying the moment, you will encourage him to go more and harder.

Give him carte blanche to tell you to do whatever he wants

Try spending a session giving your partner the authority to make any decisions that he wants. If he asks you to do something, give it a shot. Let him know that on that day, he is free to do what he wants to enjoy himself.

Pay attention to pacing

When you are speaking to your partner, you should make sure that you get the pacing right. Early on in the encounter, or during the foreplay stage, you will probably speak to each other slowly and breathily. But, as things get heated, you will probably find that your breathing has picked up and that you are likely to speak quicker.

Chapter 4: Dirty Talk for Women

Women are a bit different than men in terms of what they want to hear. While at the heart of things, they want the same thing, to feel wanted, and to feel sexy, they also do not always want to be treated like a sex object. Yes, there are plenty of women who get off on being called a slut or a whore. Yes, there are plenty of women that want you to tell them what to do or rough them up, but there are also women who prefer more subtlety in their bed.

You need to learn to approach women the right way if you want to be able to properly turn them on, and thankfully, you have this chapter. Forego any notion that your woman wants to be called a dirty slut or that she wants you to destroy her sloppy pussy. She might but let her tell you that she wants you to do that before trying to establish it yourself.

The Right Approach

When it comes to fucking and dirty talk, you need to approach it the right way if you hope to turn her on the right way. The way that you approach her or talk to her will determine if she wants to actually get down to business with you or not. If you want to make sure that you are turning her on, you need to take the right approach in the first place. This means that you must remember that really when you're not turned on, dirty talk honestly sounds a bit ridiculous. It does, and that's okay! Think about it—the act of sex itself is honestly a bit ridiculous on its own. How weird is it that sex itself is just the act of rubbing your body against someone else's because you like the feeling? From a practical or logical position, just the act of sex is strange, so is it that hard to believe that narrating out that sex would also be strange?

However, you must make sure that you take the right perspective when you are speaking to women. You should make sure that you are subtle and only as raunchy or dirty as she is comfortable with. After all, dirty talk is meant to be something that everyone is comfortable with. You must make sure that your partner is just as comfortable and happy with what is happening as you are.

There are some words that are off limits as well—don't call her bits a vagina or even a cunt, unless she wants you to. You don't need to be so formal, nor do you need to be so vulgar, especially early on. Rather, make sure that you are making use of words that you know are generally accepted. Pussy, clit, boobs, and tits will do just fine.

Talk and Touch

The most effective dirty talk is able to combine talk and touch to make the most erotic setting possible so that she will enjoy every moment of what is happening to make a sensual, sexy moment that she will love. Mix erogenous zones, the areas on the body that are particularly sensual and create sexual pleasure. Turning someone on is not limited to just being in someone else's pants—all sorts of areas throughout the body are highly sensitive, and they can create that arousal that you are looking for. Women have several different areas in the body that are likely to be delightfully stimulating, including:

- **The clitoris:** This is the most sensitive of the erogenous zones, and if you want to turn someone on and get her off, the best place to focus on is her clit. Women love the pressure and the vibrations that can be used here.
- **The vagina:** The inside of the vagina is full of nerve endings, and deep stimulation is incredibly pleasurable. However, on the outside, lighter touches tend to be preferred.
- **The cervix:** This is the bottom of the uterus and is full of its own nerve pathways that can aid a woman in reaching orgasm.
- **The mouth and lips:** Kissing is essential to a relationship, but it also aids greatly in arousal. If you want to turn your partner on, you should make sure that you are willing and ready to play with both her mouth and her lips to really get her moving.
- **The neck:** The nape of a woman's neck is highly erotic for most women, especially with a light, gentle

touch. If you want to turn her on, gently kiss at or nibble at her neck.
- **The nipples:** Nipples, when stimulated, turn on the same parts of the brain responsible for processing the clitoris and vagina. If you want to turn her on, nipple stimulation, particularly with pressure and vibrations, is a surefire way to do so.
- **The ears:** The ears on women are highly sensitive to touch, thanks to all of the nerve endings. This means that gently brushing over her ears while whispering your dirty talk into them is a fantastic way to turn her on and get her moving.

What She Wants to Hear

Women love to hear their partners making sounds. Silence says that you are not actually enjoying it at all, whether you are or not. Do your partner a favor and actually tell her what you are enjoying in the moment. Women want to hear something—*anything*—during sex, so long as you are not being offensive. Sound like you enjoy yourself, whether you are turning on the dirty talk or even just moaning or sounding like you are enjoying it. Tell her how much you like the sex or how hot she looks. Let her know how much you want to keep going or how you want her to continue. Really, so long as you are giving her positive feedback and you are making sure that you follow her boundaries, you are likely to get some pretty good feedback from her as well. She wants to know that she can feel wanted and desired. She wants to feel like you are having a good time.

Really, just about anything can be sexy if you know what you are doing and how you are talking to her. Follow her cues. Make sure that you are mindful of what she seems comfortable with as well, and don't lose sight that you are talking to her to turn her on, not for yourself. If you can do that, you are likely to have far more luck.

Phrases for Dirty Talk with Women

- You are so fucking gorgeous
- I love what you are doing with your [hand, mouth, pussy, etc.]
- How does that feel?
- I'm going to fill you up
- I want you so bad
- Cum for me
- I'm going to take you
- Your pussy feels so tight right now
- You taste good
- Do you like that?
- I need you right now

Dirty Talk During Foreplay

During foreplay, you have the benefit of being able to talk to her and turn her on. Much like men, she wants to hear you talk about what you want to do or what you *need* to do. Urgency is hot, and women want to hear that from you. If you can make it clear to her that you need her right that moment, you are going to get her wet. You can tell her that you want to do something to her with that urgent, quiet tone, and she will either oblige or ask you to do something else instead.

If you tell her that you are ready to fuck her, or you are able to tell her things that you want to do, you can get her ready in advance. You create that anticipation; you are fostering that sexual tension that will ensure that the big moment will be even better. Remember, women don't want to fuck someone that is disinterested. They want to be wanted, just like men do. They want to feel like they are desired and attractive. They want to feel like their partner is having a good time so that they are able to have a good time, and the sooner that you can make that good time happen, the better. You just have to know what you are doing and how to do it.

During foreplay, try telling her what you intend to do or what you wish that you could do. It will turn her on, and she may even follow through with it if you tell her that you want it enough. If you want to make sure that she's hot for you, you need to make sure that you make her believe that you want her first. There is not much that is hotter than being wanted in the first place.

Dirty Talk During Sex

During sex, things aren't much different—you want to make sure that you are talking to your partner and telling her just how much that you actually want her. Make her believe that you do genuinely want to enjoy her body and let her know how good she feels. Boost her confidence. Tell her that you are so happy with how she is feeling around you as you thrust into her so that she knows that you are enjoying it. Moan a bit. Let her hear just how much you enjoy it.

In the moment, women want to hear that they are good in bed. They want to feel like they are actually bringing you pleasure so that they can enjoy that pleasure as well, and the best way to ensure that that can happen is if you tell them. Of course, you want to tow that line carefully and make sure that what you are doing is something that they are comfortable with. You should always be willing to listen if someone says that something bothers them and make sure that you correct yourself if you continue to try to use that language in the future as well.

Tips for Dirty Talk for Women
Be tactful

Make sure that when you are using dirty talk, you do so tactfully. Make sure that you use it in situations that make sense or that call for it. This means that if you are having a serious conversation about something, you don't tell her that you wish that your hands were on her tits instead of listening to her.

Tell her when you're cumming

Women want to know when you're about to finish. Especially if they are on top, they don't want to continue bouncing away after you're done. Let them know when you're done so that they can accommodate.

Say her name

Just like with men, women want to hear their partners say their name. It is validating, and that acknowledgment brings great pleasure. It can elevate the eroticism of your sex and make it so much better just by dropping her name in there somewhere. Whether you mention her name, or you quietly moan her name to her as she rides you, making sure that you use her name is a great way to make her feel validated.

Sound like you are enjoying it

Make sure that when you are fucking, you sound like you are actually, well, fucking. Your silence is usually taken as being distracted or uninterested. It is far better for everyone involved if you sound like you genuinely enjoy it. Don't be embarrassed by any sounds that you might make—she'll find them attractive and enjoyable.

Tell her she's good in bed

When you tell her that she's good in bed, she'll feel validated and confident enough to want to continue fucking or to want to fuck in the first place. If you tell her how much you're looking forward to having sex and you specify why, you will find that you give her that much-needed confidence boost that will take you far.

Tell her in the moment what she is doing that you like

If she suddenly does something that is particularly enjoyable, such as using her tongue a certain way or touching you or kissing you a specific way, you can tell her that you like it. If you like it, tell her so she can do it again. She will find more enjoyment in the fact that you have complimented her as well.

Check in with her during sex

Ask her if she likes what you are doing, or if she needs you to do something else. See if there are ways that you can change what you are doing to make sure that you are tending to her every need as well. She will also feel more attracted to you when you clearly make it a point to check in with her to make sure that she is enjoying things.

Ask her what she wants you to do to finish her off

When it comes to it, you should make sure that you ask her what she wants, especially to get off with. You want to make sure that you satisfy her completely, and that means that you need communication. When you can feel that she's getting close, you can ask her what she wants you to do to finish her off. Sometimes, it is just that act of caring for her that can make her crave to be with you even more.

Set boundaries

If you are going to be sexual with someone else, make sure that you tell her that she can set a boundary without question. You can tell her that if she is uncomfortable with something, she should tell you. You want to make sure that she is able to tell you when you do cross a boundary. This makes her feel safe, and when she is safe and comfortable, she is going to be willing to unleash the sexual individual within her. If she feels like she is comfortable with you, she will feel like she can continue to be intimate with you and that she can push those boundaries and experiment with you, knowing that she can stop you if she ever feels uncomfortable.

Tell her she smells good

Let's face it—sex is kind of gross if you think about it. There are exchanges of fluids. You are kissing and in each other's faces. You are breathing on each other and getting sweaty as you fuck. She may be feeling a bit self-conscious during the act, but if you tell her that you love the way that she smells, you are letting her know that she is not gross. You are letting her know that she is attractive to you, and that will help her to unwind a bit and enjoy the moment more.

Tell her she's sexy

It can help greatly to tell her just how attractive and sexy that she is. Let her know how much you love to fuck her so that she can feel like she is confident enough to keep moving forward and to keep engaging with you.

Tell her you want to continue all night long

You can also make sure that you tell her that you want to continue your romp all night long to make her feel like she is the most important thing to you. You are effectively convincing her that she is your utmost priority and that above all else, you want her. You tell her that she is not competing against video games, friends, drinking, or anything else—you want her and her alone, and that is erotic.

Tell her to talk dirty to you

If you tell her to dirty talk with you, you will help inspire her further. You can get her to engage more with you when you do this, and that is a major turn on as well. Use this to really get her involved and to make her go crazy. After all, sex is a two-way street—you both have to be involved and engaged if you want the best possible sex.

Follow this pattern

Dirty talk doesn't have to be crass or aggressive—it can be affectionate with a long-term partner or a spouse as well. You can follow this simple strategy to make sure that you are giving the best possible dirty talk that you can: "It feels amazing when you [action] my [body part]" or "Your [body part] is so amazing, I want to [action] them." If you can follow this pattern, you will be able to compliment more than just her sex—you compliment her as a whole, and that is incredibly validating.

Be urgent

Very little is more of a turn on than being needed by someone. If you want to make someone want you, you make it clear that you *need* them. This works with women as well. Urgency is hot. If you want to make her wet, let her know how much you need her. Your voice should be almost a plea—like you need her more than anything else.

Tell her she tastes good

If you are going down on her, let her know that you like how her pussy tastes. It makes her feel like you want to be down in her pussy, pleasing her.

Moan

If you want her, tell her without needing to say a word. As you play with her, let her know just how badly you need her without a single word. Just a well-placed moan can say it all.

Tell her how hard/wet you are

If you have a penis, tell her how hard it is for her. If you have a vagina, tell her how dripping wet it is for her. She will love to hear how your body is working for her and how she is impacting the way that you are able to move and interact. She wants to know that she is ultimately

Comment on how wet she is

As you play with her, you can make mention of just how wet she is and how that makes you feel as well. You can tell her just how hot you think it is that she is as wet as she is so that she can feel a bit more confident about herself as well. Tell her just how enjoyable you find it.

Comment on how tight she is

Whether she is tight around your finger or your cock, let her know. Tell her just how much you like the feeling and how much you want to enjoy it. Comment on the feeling that you have around you and how great it is.

Tell her which position you want her in and what you are about to do to her

When you take charge like this, you will probably set her on fire. Most people enjoy being wanted so desperately that the other person is demanding that they do something. Of course, you must make sure that you are still respecting any boundaries that ought to be respected but let her know what you want.

Tell her how much you want her

Doting on her in the moment, saying just how badly you want her pussy around you, or to taste her on your lips, is going to set her off. It is highly erotic to be the object of someone's sexual attention, especially if there is a mutual attraction there.

Tell her how beautiful she looks in that position

Whether it is from behind, from above, or below, tell her just how great she looks to you in the moment as you are fucking her. She will eat it up.

Experiment until you find what you both like

Take some time to figure out what it is that you both want out of your relationship. Every now and then, in the moment, try something new and see if she responds well to it. She may love what you are doing, or she may wish that you would not do that ever again. Either way, you can get to know each other and what you both want better over time.

Tease her

All day long, tell her how much you want to enjoy her. Make her want you and let that tension build all day long. There is nothing better than making sure that the sexual tension is running high so that you will be able to take advantage of all of that pent up energy later on.

Tell her not to do something because it's turning you on

This goes right back to teasing. If she's walking around the store with you, you can lean over and whisper in her ears that if she keeps walking like that, you're going to have to do something about it at home because she's driving you wild. Of course, she'll then most likely do it more to drive you crazy too.

Tell her that you want to dominate her/have her dominate you

Depending upon the perspective that you take, you can either make her in charge, or you can choose to dominate over her. There is something about being in complete control, or alternatively, to giving someone else complete control, that can be a great turn on, especially when you and your partner are on the same page.

Tell her to scream for you

If you feel like she's getting a bit too lost in the moment, you can escalate by asking her to get loud for you, encouraging her to scream for you. Of course, you should be mindful of neighbors with this method.

Make her think about you by talking about how turned on she makes you

Even if you are not actively having sex in the moment, you can tell her all about how distracted you get when you think about her. She'll then be thinking about you thinking about her.

Tell her just how intoxicating you find her

Women love being doted on, and especially if you are trying to warm her up without just getting everything flowing right that moment, you can try telling her something about how enticing and intoxicating she is. Tell her the smell of her hair is mind-blowing, or that she looks absolutely divine and that you can't keep your eyes off of her. Tell her just how attracted you are to her and that you can't stop looking/smelling/thinking about her.

Chapter 5: Digital Dirty Talk

We live in a digital age—there is no way around it. That means that you need to stop and consider that you are no longer stuck talking to each other. You don't just have to talk to each other in person anymore. You have the internet in the pocket of your pants these days—you have an ability to communicate at will if you want it. All you have to do is pull it out of your pocket and use it. That's right, your phone is the greatest facilitator of foreplay and sexing when it comes to turning on your partner with ease. All you need to do is make sure that you know how to write the best sext you can. As you read here, we are going to be looking at how to sext, how to pace things, and how to overcome the initial awkwardness of what you are doing. We will also talk about the importance of being able to take a picture that is enticing but not too revealing, as well as several tips to help you.

How to Sext

Sexting makes one of the greatest forms of foreplay, which you can use just about anywhere at any time. So long as you are mindful of your phone, you can simply send messages back and forth all day long, building up that anticipation and making sure that both you and your partner are driving each other wild. You can tell them all of the fantasies that you have throughout your time. You can tell your partner what you want them to do, or what you want to do to them. You can make sure that you are taking the time to drive them insane as well. When you play your cards right, you can keep that sex desire on their mind all day long, and that means that when you finally are able to come together again, you can enjoy all of that passion again.

Sexting does not have to be difficult or challenging. However, there are a few considerations to keep in mind. You want to make sure that you follow a few rules so that you avoid running into other problems.

Mind the timing

Make sure that you are well aware of what your partner's schedule looks like so you do not send them a message when they are in a place where it would be considered inappropriate. While technically just about any time would be inappropriate, it is important to keep in mind that your partner may be busy at work when you sext them, or they may be with family or other people that should not be exposed to that. Rather than just sending a sexy picture, try coming up with a code word. Ask your partner if they are busy before you do anything at all.

Be slow

Make sure that when you are sexting your partner, you mind the fact that your conversation should move slowly. You don't want to just go from 0 to 60 in an instant—rather, you want to make sure that you start slow and that you want to play. Talk about how much you enjoyed the other night or send a subtly suggestive picture.

Stay within your comfort zone

Make sure that, no matter what, you work within your comfort zone. Your sexting doesn't need to be explicit—you can even just send a message saying that you're ready to have fun with your partner, or you can send pictures of yourself masturbating if you really wanted to. You should start slowly and make sure that you are comfortable with where the sexting is going at any point in time.

Always send a warning before nudes

If you are going to send a picture that's not safe for work, give them that warning. You don't want them to get in trouble at work if your nude popped up on their lock screen, nor do you want them to open the message with others around or within sight of your picture.

Have fun

Remember, the whole point of dirty talk and sexting is to have fun and to encourage that sexual tension that will help you to really enjoy the moment. This means that you should enjoy the entire time that you are sexting. You can even draw your inspiration from porn, erotica, and romance novels.

Details matter

When you are sexting, the details are where the bulk of your content is. You need to make sure that you are actively encouraging each other to provide yourselves with the right amount of details. If you can nail that, you will be just fine.

Pacing for Good Digital Dirty Talk

Just like with sex, good digital dirty talk and sexting needs to be just the right pacing, or you are going to run into all sorts of problems. If you want to make sure that you are able to turn your partner on without anything else happening, you want to make sure that you understand the right pacing. You should always start slow at first and build up. When you are just getting started, you should make sure that you lead into it. Talk about how much you miss the other person or that you're thinking of them. Send a few suggestive emojis or a picture that is suggestive, but not revealing.

Think of good digital dirty talk as being quite like sex—you build up to the big moment. You talk about fucking each other and about enjoying it. You go over what it is that you want from each other, enacting fantasies. Think of the following exchange:

I'm thinking of you.

Really? I was thinking about the other night just now. I really liked what you did with your tongue.

Mmm, yeah, I'd like to do that again. I want to kiss and tease you up until you're shaking and begging for more.

Yes, please. I want to feel you tonight.

I can come over and then we can cum over together ;)

Notice how it is not particularly explicit right off the bat. It's teasing, light, and suggestive. It is not meant to be highly explicit at first. It is something that is supposed to build up that tension so that when you are together, you have enough of that tension built up that you can't keep your hands off of each other. Whether you are sexting as your own personal porn as you masturbate or if you are sexting just to build up that tension, you are making sure that you and your partner are ready to go.

Overcoming Awkwardness of Digital Dirty Talk

Sexting can be a bit awkward if you don't know what you are doing, but don't let that deter you. Too many people think, "Wow, I'm not creative enough for this, or I can't think of anything to say." However, that doesn't mean that you can't enjoy it. Sexting can be great. It can be fun and playful while also being erotic. You don't have to start out too explicitly, nor do you ever have to go further than you want to. Start out slowly and work your way up to what you want. If getting a text that says, "This is waiting for you," and a picture of a hard cock is a turn off for you, say something. Make it clear that that is not working for you.

The best way to overcome the awkwardness is honestly just to get started and make it happen. Even if for you it is a compliment or a vague reference to that last time that you and your partner did something highly erotic, that is still something. Even a message as innocent as "I miss your lips on mine," can be erotic. It tells them what you want in that moment and is also an invitation for your partner to take control.

You can also ask questions that can lead to the fantasies and sexually explicit messages that you want. Ask your partner what they are thinking about in the moment to open up the conversation. Ask them what their fantasy is and let them take control. This can eliminate some of the awkwardness for yourself as well.

Consider these different options to start up your conversation with your partner that are able to skip that initial awkwardness:

- I want you to keep me warm
- I'm thinking about you
- What are you up to right now?
- Your lips on my [body part] feel so great
- I miss your hands on my [body part]
- When's the last time you thought about me?
- I'm getting wet/hard thinking about you right now
- Want to try something new tonight?

Taking the Perfect Picture

Taking the perfect picture is important to your sexting life, and the best ways that you can make that happen typically involve having some fun and finding just the right angles. Keep in mind that when you take your pictures, a lot of the time, less is more. When you are trying to choose the right photo, try taking several and looking through them until you can find the right angles for you. Every person has their own angles that make them look amazing—it is just a matter of figuring out where they are.

Start by making sure that you know your angles. This is one time where selfie sticks can be your greatest asset. Make sure that you experiment regularly and that you remember that natural lighting can be a great asset as well. Your pictures do not have to be revealing. They do not have to be anything other than suggestive. You could post a picture of your thighs without taking off your skirt. You could show your cleavage without revealing any nipple. If you are a man, you could show some abs or a toned arm without ever taking off your pants.

You can also work by making your phone your partner. Instead of trying to take a photo just right, you can focus on the image as if your phone itself is your partner, engaging in what is effectively POV pictures that will create that image of your partner being your phone. You will put your picture in the position that you would prefer your partner and then get into the right position, looking right at the camera.

With the right angles and the right attitude, you can usually figure out exactly what it is that you should be doing. Take a whole bunch of pictures and then make sure that the ones that you choose are the right angles and that they make you look great. If you can do that, you will find that you can take the sexiest pictures with ease.

What Not to Do during Sexting

Of course, if you are sexting, there are a few things that you should absolutely avoid at all costs to make sure that ultimately, you are doing the right thing at the right time. Make sure that you keep the following in mind so that you avoid common mistakes that can be problematic.

- **Don't send unwanted photos:** Regardless of whether you are a man or a woman, avoid the unsolicited nudes, especially if you haven't told them that you intend to send any.
- **Don't send photos to someone that you can't trust:** If you have just started dating someone or you can't trust the person that you are dating, don'ts end them any photos.
- **Don't take things too seriously:** Remember, sexting is supposed to be fun. Don't take it too seriously and enjoy the time that you spend teasing your partner.

Tips for Digital Dirty Talk

Offer up something that you want to do

What's sexier than detailing out exactly what you intend to do with your partner? Send them a message with you telling them exactly what you will be doing the next time that you all get together.

Be detailed

Remember that in sexting, all of the details are what do the talking. In engaging with sex, you are able to lead with your body, but in sexting, you must lead with your words instead.

Talk about dreams

Spend some time telling your partner all about a dream that you just had so that your partner can understand just how much you like or are thinking about him or her.

Tell them that you're in the shower

This invites them to text you with all sorts of different things, from what they will do to you when they see you, just imagining you naked and fresh out of the shower.

Be honest

Tell them exactly what you've felt so that they have the opportunity to reciprocate if they want to. This can open up all sorts of fun sexting ideas, and all you have to do is tell them about what it is that you want.

Have your partner turn off image previews

Make sure that your partner is not going to have your sexy picture plastered on his screen in public areas where it could be embarrassing for both of you. If you intend to sext with each other, make sure that your images and messages will not be on display for the world to see at a glance.

Turn on the heat

You can tell them that you are fantasizing about them right there in the moment and ask what they think about what you are saying. This is a great way to turn them on and get them engaging with you.

Express your regret that they're not there with you

This is a great way for you to tell them that you are disappointed that, at the end of the day, they are not present with you. This could take the place of saying something along the lines of, "Man, I wish you were here," to "It's too bad that you're not here right now."

Ask them to guess what you are thinking about

You should also try asking them what they think that is on your mind right at that moment. From being excited about how you are thinking about them, to all of the fun you intend to have encouraged, to guess what is on your mind, and then share whether they are right or not.

Let them know what you are wearing

Or not wearing. Tell them what you have on and ask what they want to do with you. They will probably want to tantalizingly remove each and every item that you are wearing

Ask them to take you

Because you will be in a position where you can say just about anything, try asking them to take you. You would be surprised at the results that you get when they think that all you want is a good, hard fuck, especially if that is you telling them the truth.

Only send messages that you feel comfortable sharing

Unfortunately, a few bad apples tend to ruin things for everyone, and sexting is yet another example of exactly that. Too many people have been burned by trying to sext, only to have their images plastered up online or disbursed among people. This is a major problem, and you want to nip it in the bud so that it cannot be a problem. Don't let anyone pressure you into sending messages that you don't want to send.

Tempt them with previews

Give them a quick sneak peek of everything that you intend to do to them as soon as they get home or to your place. If you intend to drop his pants as soon as he walks in the door and you tell him that, make sure that you are willing to follow through with it.

Play with the senses

Sure, you're apart, but that doesn't mean that you have to ignore the sense of touch, taste, or smell. You can entice each and every sense with the words that you type onto your phone and send off to him or her, and there is a good chance that using those words will drive him insane.

Make a request

These requests can be kind or demanding—you can ask politely for something, or you can tell them that you need them right that moment and that you can't wait any longer to get your hands on them.

Tease them
Tell them vaguely what you are doing or thinking about, only to make them wait a bit before you respond. This will drive them crazy, wondering what they are going to get back from you.

Send a quick video for them

If you are feeling especially brave, send a quick message with a video showing what you are doing to yourself. It could be a quick preview of you masturbating, or even your big O moment to drive the other person wild.

Reminisce about sex that was amazing

Tell them something that they did that you are thinking about at that moment. Talk about how much you miss that moment and what it made you think or feel.

Compliment them

Tell them what they did that you really enjoyed recently and just how much it impressed you. By sending compliments sometimes, you can usually get your partner to start thinking about that time, which of course, is a turn on.

Thank them for something

Sometimes, what they have done is so memorable to you that you need to send them a quick thank you message. Telling them that you appreciate what they have done sexually is a great way to validate them and turn them on quicker.

Come up with your responses for when you're not sure what to say back

Sometimes, you will get a message that you're unsure about how you should respond. When that happens, try saying something like, "wow, that turns me on so much," or "Tell me more." When you encourage them to keep talking, you are engaging even if you don't know what you should be saying back.

Have a roleplay session

You can sext a roleplay. You can write out what you are doing, in your mind, of course, and the other party can reply to you with what they do in response. You might not be able to touch each other, but you can write out your fantasies with each other and imagine it all happening, driving each other insane as you do so.

Be adventurous

Make sure that when you are talking to your partner, you are adventurous. If there was ever a time to pursue and explore your sexuality, it would be during the time in which you are able to engage digitally without any pressure of following through physically. If you discover that you don't like it, then you don't like it, and that's that.

Send pictures

Even if you just send something suggestive, go for it and see what happens, especially if you've talked about doing so in the past. People are visual creatures, and it can be highly erotic to see the impact that you have on someone else's body when they're not expecting it.

Get creative with the language

Make sure that when you are messaging him, you keep in mind that you can only say cock and pussy so much before it is time to change things up. Try to get creative, or even poetic sometimes. You might find that somethings that strikes them the right way and gets them to do what you want more than anything else.

Remember it's a conversation

When you are sexting someone, remember that it is a two-way conversation. You should be paying attention to the way that you engage with the other person and let him or her have some fun getting to talk. Remember that you should both be engaging with each other rather than anything else.

Use sexting as a precursor to dirty talk

Dirty talk in person can be quite awkward, but ultimately, it can be a great way for you to practice talking about what you want and a great exercise in communication that will help to ensure that you are able to talk in the moment as well. You can tell them exactly what you want—tell them that you want them to suck you off or tease you or fuck you via text and, eventually, work up to saying it in person as well.

Be ready to take it live

At some point, be ready to take what is being said live. Your sext session may very quickly turn into wanting to actually video chat or even meet up quickly to see what is going on.

Check in afterward

After sex, you have the ability to cuddle with each other or spoon or enjoy the moment. That is not quite so easy to do when you are engaging in sexting just due to the fact that you aren't close enough. However, you can take the time to check in with the other person and make sure that they recognize that they should be mindful of how they are interacting.

Ask your partner what turns them on

This is a great way to get them thinking about what it is that you can do for them, which not only helps you to know how to address a sexting session but will also ensure that you are able to address those needs in person as well.

Ask what they like you to do or like about you

You want to make sure that you are involving your partner and letting them choose what it is that turns them on. Have them tell you what it is about you that drives them crazy.

Chapter 6: What NOT to Do

Of course, when it comes to dirty talk and sexting, it is important that you pay attention to some pretty important things that should never be done. As you read through this chapter, you are going to be introduced to several things that you should just never do when you are using dirty talk. Make sure that you communicate what it is that you want to do and how you can make it happen as well. You want to make sure that when it comes right down to it, your partner knows what it is that will turn you on more than anything, but you also need to know what not to do.

If you go too far too quickly with dirty talk in general, you can cause some serious problems. You could, for example, completely ruin the sexual relationship entirely. You can destroy any trust that is had or any respect that is necessary for a mutually consensual relationship, and let's be honest here—no one wants to do that. For that reason, it is highly important for you to take the time to communicate what you want, boundaries, and understand what not to do.

This list will provide you with thirty things that you should *never* do in dirty talk. Of course, there will always be the occasional exception to the rule, but if you pay attention to what not to do, you can usually make sure that you and your partner are on the same page enough to ensure that neither of you are hurting the other.

Escalating too quickly

Remember that you can't go from 0 to 60 without first stopping and asking what the other person wants. If it is your first encounter with this person, don't start it off by calling her a dirty little slut with a pussy that needs to be punished for being so sloppy. You could *try* to do that, but there is a very real, very good chance that doing so is going to create a major problem for you and your relationship. Instead, try focusing on what you can do to slowly bring up the heat of what you are saying to what you want it to be. Start slowly and avoid moving too quickly.

Not going far enough

On the other hand, if you are super sterile about what you are saying, you won't turn anyone on at all. You need to be able to follow that bridge between too much and not enough if you want to be able to convince your partner that you really do want him or her. If your voice is flat or you are not talking at all, you may tell the other person that you're just not interested, even if that is not actually the case at all.

Timing it wrong

Make sure that when you are reaching out or using dirty talk, your timing is right. If you are in the middle of a conversation with someone, don't suddenly completely change the mood, especially if the initial communication was there because of the way that you are feeling in the moment. You need to be able to understand that ultimately, there is a time and place for everything.

Not being believable

Make sure that when you talk to your partner, you make it believable. It is not believable to say that you've been jerking it for the last three hours when you are at work, for example, nor is it believable that you would walk around work for three hours pitching a tent. Make sure that whatever you say, you make it believable so that your partner is just as turned on as you are.

Making it seem rehearsed

You also should make sure that you avoid making any attempts to interact with your partner seem too rehearsed. You can't tell your partner the exact same line that you have rehearsed and repeated over and over again and hope that they will listen. If things seem too automatic, you have a very real chance of simply offending the other person rather than actually making any good, clear progress with what you are attempting to do. It is always more important to be honest and realistic than anything else.

Making it too complicated

Dirty talk doesn't have to be complicated, nor should it be. You need to make sure that any dirty talk that you are using is going to be effective and usable without having to worry too much about repercussions. When you are able to talk dirty to someone else, it should not be super complicated, nor should it be full of all sorts of attempts to make you seem smarter or try-hard than you actually would normally be.

Not personalizing it enough

Another common mistake that people make are making their dirty talk too impersonal. Yes, you can say the same thing to just about anyone, but are they all going to respond the same way? Are they all really going to appreciate the way that you have chosen to approach them? Many people find that they are far happier if they are able to have any dirty talk personalized. Instead of just saying, "Fuck me harder," you can figure out how to personalize it—"I love the way you're riding me with that thick cock of yours," for example. Now you are getting specific and personalizing, which allows for more connection and, therefore, more intimacy as well. You need to be able to keep that line just right between not enough and just enough.

Making your partner uncomfortable with it

You should always make sure that you are able to keep your partner comfortable during dirty talk, and this means that you and your partner must have some very serious talks about boundaries to make sure that you are both able to follow along and be comfortable. Of course, this also means that you both will need to be willing to talk about boundaries so that neither of you are unintentionally pushing things too far one way or another.

Repeating back what your partner has said

Even if your partner has just said the sexiest thing imaginable, there is no reason to repeat it back to them. Don't tell them exactly what they just said to you unless you want them to stop and look at you like you completely missed the point. Make sure that you are telling them things that are new and unique to make sure that they are able to understand that you are, in fact, attempting to turn them on, not to make a complete fool out of yourself as you go.

Any mention of pregnancy or making babies

Especially if you and your partner are not exclusive or are not long-term partners, you should leave out any talk of babies. If it is a casual fuck session with your booty call, you should not be telling them that you can't wait to put babies into them. No matter how hot it may seem in the moment, all you are doing is setting your partner up for expectations that are unreasonable and also making it a point to completely avoid the way that you should be interacting. Parenthood is not sexy. While some people revel in it, especially the first year, sex drives can tank, and when that happens, you don't want to be talking about putting a baby into someone else. Likewise, you should not tell your partner that you want them to put a baby in you, either.

Leave food out of it

Unless this is something that the two of you have discussed, don't refer to his or her bits as food objects. Most people don't find calling someone's penis a sausage particularly attractive. It is problematic for most people, in fact, and you can run into all sorts of issues if you are not mindful of the way that you approach the situation. Instead, just leave food where it belongs—in the kitchen and out of your bedroom life.

There is a time and place to be romantic and sweet

Keep in mind that there is absolutely a time for romance and being sweet—and that is rarely during active fucking. Recognize that there is a major difference between fucking, which is usually regarded as almost animalistic in the way that it is used and being willing to sensually make love to someone else. If you are fucking, don't whisper sweet nothings into your partner's ear. If you are making love, don't tell her that her pussy is so tight and wet. Know the difference between romantic sex and passion, no strings or emotions attached sex, and adjust accordingly.

Don't discuss bodily fluids

The only bodily fluids that have a place in your sex life are ejaculate and the lubricant that vaginas make. Don't tell your partner that you want to pee on them, especially if you are just starting out, and you don't know his or her kinks yet. You need to take the time to get to know them and make your actions accordingly. It is only then when you are careful about what you are doing that you can make that appropriate progress. Leave out urine, spit, and any other fluids unless explicitly discussed and agreed to in advance.

Leave the exes out of it

There is nothing worse than enjoying the moment only to suddenly be compared to an ex, whether being better or worse. No matter whether the comment is meant as a compliment or not, you do not want to think that your partner is busy comparing you to see how you stand up against your ex-boyfriend or girlfriend. That's a great way to set up all sorts of resentment and concern that things are going to go wrong if you are not careful. Instead, pay close attention to the ways that you engage with your partner and make sure that you are choosing to give them the respect that they deserve without worrying about the exes that are involved.

Don't make your dirty talk or sexting scenario too impossible

If you are sexting or dirty talking someone else, unless you have both agreed to do some roleplay, don't make your situation suddenly so fantastic that it will take away from the moment. This means don't suddenly be fucking your partner on another planet or something. Make it believable and call it good. This is one of the most important things that you can do to make sure that you are being effective with your small talk. You must make it believable and enjoyable.

Avoid making puns, no matter how tempting

It happens to the best of us at some point in time—that pun comes to mind, and it's really hard to resist saying it. However, keep in mind that when you are using puns with people, you keep those puns out of the bedroom. Most people won't find it attractive if you suddenly drop a pun off of something that you were enjoying just moments prior, and you can completely destroy the moment if you are not careful.

Make sure that you don't say something ridiculous

Similarly, try to avoid anything that is too ridiculous as you are fucking. This is not the time or place for that. Rather, this is the time and place for you to enjoy the moment. Avoid making any jokes at all during this period of time and try to keep your talking as serious as possible in the moment. Say things that are sexy. Don't say things that are going to be annoying, silly, or potentially kill the mood.

Listen to the suggestions that your partner makes

If your partner asks you to do something, you should do it. Make sure that you are regularly doing what your partner has requested of you so that you are able to figure out what it is that you need to do to get the most enjoyment for both of you. After all, if you want him to come back for seconds, or you want her to beg you for it, you are going to want to make sure that your sex is memorable enough for you to want to do it again. The best way to get that memorable nature is to make sure that you are doing whatever your partner has suggested.

Don't be too derogatory (at first)

Unless explicitly told that it is okay to call your partner's vagina a dirty, slutty cunt, you probably shouldn't do it. Especially if your relationship is still new and you are still getting to know each other, you do not want to unintentionally make things worse by saying the wrong things, and the easiest way to push too far is to use derogatory language that is going to turn everyone off from the situation. Rather than giving in to that derogatory language, you should instead consider having a genuine conversation about what it is that you and your partner both want.

Don't tell them to be quiet

If your partner is starting to moan or really enjoy the moment, one of the worst things that you can do is tell him or her to be quiet because they are distracting you. Instead of looking at their moans of pleasure as distractions, consider seeing them for what they are—clear signs that you are doing a good job because the other person literally cannot control the sounds that they are making in that moment. If you were to tell them to quiet down, all you would do is make them feel self-conscious or even make them feel like the relationship not worth continuing.

Don't try to convince the other party to skip the condom

All too often, you will hear men try to get out of wearing a condom during sex. However, that is not only bad practice because you can unintentionally end up pregnant, it is also dangerous if you are not in a committed relationship with someone that you trust. There is no place in dirty talk for risky, potentially dangerous sex, and because of that, do not even try to convince your partner that you do not need a condom. Newsflash—you *do* need a condom, and you *do* need to make sure that you are wearing it the right way.

Don't be too anatomically correct

While it is important to make sure that you are not being too vulgar, you also shouldn't overcorrect—do not tell her that you want to put your penis in between her labia and thrust into her vaginal cavity. That's not sexy. At all. Instead, make sure that you stick to generally acceptable terms. Cock and pussy, for example, are pretty regularly respected and acceptable. However, terms like cunt are debatable for many and should be avoided unless she specifically tells you to call it a cunt.

Don't dwell on something that upsets the other party

If you make a mistake in the moment, it's okay—it happens to the best of us. However, unless you have seriously triggered your partner, you don't have to suddenly stop what you're doing. Rather, you can offer a quick apology and keep on moving forward unless your partner shows signs of wanting to stop. This means that there is no real reason for you to be rejecting everything that you're doing. There is no real reason for you to stop everything to suddenly apologize repeatedly and have a long, drawn out conversation, especially if the other party shows no desire to have one at that moment. You can revisit later if you really want to make sure that you have that conversation.

Don't ask if they are faking things

One of the worst things that you can do in the moment is to accuse your partner of faking something. Your partner should be trustworthy, and you should be able to feel like, if your partner is saying something to you, they mean it. Don't act like your partner is lying to you just because you think that they are being unrealistic. If you are worried about them being truthful, you probably shouldn't be pursuing that relationship in the first place.

Don't criticize your partner's bodies

It should go without saying that during sex or sexual play unless explicitly told otherwise, there is no real room for insulting the body of another person. Unless you have both discussed the idea of playing with degrading each other, there is a high likelihood that you are just going to upset each other and create all sorts of major problems. It is better to leave the degradation out of all dirty talk until you and your partner have had that candid discussion. While some people live by, it is better to ask forgiveness than permission; you can destroy your sexual relationship in this manner relatively simply. Don't even bother risking it—it isn't worth it.

Don't bring up dirty talk during a sensual, romantic sex session

Remember that sometimes, if your session is sensual and romantic, it is best to leave the dirty talk out of it—the aggressive kind, anyway. Rather, focus on the moment, and instead of degrading comments, you should be shifting into talk of how much you are enjoying yourselves, how much you care for each other, and how you enjoy the other person's body. Aggressive dirty talk has no place if you are attempting to woo someone else.

Don't call yourself daddy unless the other party has expressed an interest

Daddy is probably one of the more controversial names that you can call your partner during sex. Some people love it, and others hate it—you kind of have to go with the flow to make it work for you. If you want to be called daddy, then let your partner know and ask how she feels. Likewise, if you want to call him daddy, you should ask in advance. Some people find it a turn on, but others may find that it is a bit weird for them, especially if he already has children that refer to him as daddy. That can be something that is pushing the agenda too far and will get all sorts of backlash. Consider having a discussion about this prior to letting it be used. This is the best interest for everyone involved, and if you don't want to ruin the moment, you will ask first

Don't try to push boundaries when they have been set

While expressing desperation for sex can be hot, begging to do something that your partner has already said that they would not do is a huge turn off. Maybe she doesn't want to have anal sex—that's her right. You can ask her, but if she says no, it is best for you to drop the point altogether. However, if you start to push the point after you have already said no, you are making a big mistake. You will probably turn him or her off quicker than anything else if you continue to push a point that has already been answered. Remember, healthy sex is all about consent, and that consent must not be coerced.

Don't talk about family in bed

Finally, make sure that talks bout real life, such as family, friends, work, or anything else, are left out of the bedroom during sex. Nothing can turn off your dirty talk game quicker than mentioning that your mother is bothering you again. Instead, you should make sure that any interactions that you have with your partner are carefully crafted. Make sure that your interactions are focused on your partner rather than other concerns or problems that may be arising. Are those problems serious? Sure—but they also shouldn't be overwhelming so much so that you are unable or unwilling to have good sex because of them. Be all in or all out, but don't drag your partner down with talks of what your family is doing or why your job is currently driving you crazy.

Chapter 7: Bonus Tips to Spice Up the Bedroom

Congratulations! You've made it through the book and know now how you can begin to implement dirty talk. However, you may be wondering what else you can do to spice up your bedroom life now that you have a pretty solid idea of what to do and what not to do. Thankfully, you are in the right spot, and as you read through this chapter, you will be introduced to all sorts of information that is going to help you really spice up that sex life without much of a hassle at all. All you need to do is make sure that you know what you are doing and how to do it so that you can enjoy your bedroom and your partner. Now, let's take a look at some more tips that you can use to ensure that your bedroom life is never lacking what you are looking for.

Sexy daddy roleplay

Roleplay is a great way that you will be able to spice up your bedroom, and you can do it with dirty talk. You can talk to your partner about a way that you would like to explore. A common one is with daddy roleplay, where one person is the daddy, and the other is the daughter. You can make use of all sorts of dirty talk as you talk to each other, talking in a completely different context. It can really spice things up when you make use of new scenarios in which you and your partner are going to be able to make sure that you and your partner are able to get off together with that dirty talk. Talk to each other about your boundaries and see if that is something that you are interested in trying. It may not be for everyone, but some people love it.

Sexy delivery roleplay

Along a similar vein, a lot of people enjoy spicing things up with other roleplays as well. A common one is pretending to have your partner deliver a pizza. Maybe you have your partner go out to pick up your favorite pizza, and when he comes back home with it, he knocks on your door, and… you don't have any money! You can't find your cash and realize that you have no way to pay for it. However, with dirty talk and the power of being able to seduce your partner, because you happened to be nude with nothing but a robe on when your partner knocked, you are able to seduce him to pay it back.

As you have fun in this way, you can add in all sorts of dirty talk, making a game out of it that you can both get off to. He can call you his little slut for putting out for pizza, and you can rock his world by getting into a role that is completely different than the one that you typically lead. After all, he is not calling you a slut; he is calling the character the slut. You may also consider getting a bit rougher than usual as well, of course respecting any boundaries that have been requested so that you and your partner can both have the best possible time with each other.

Sexy teacher roleplay

Another roleplay idea that is ripe for the dirty talk is the idea of a teacher and a student. One of you can be the newbie virgin that has never had sex before, while the other is responsible for teaching the first one everything that he or she knows about having an awesome sex life. If you want to make sure that you and your partner get the most out of this exercise, introduce all sorts of dirty talk and molding one character to match what the other character is requesting. There can be all sorts of eroticism added in if you have one person pretending to be completely new to sex while the other then gets to do all of the leading. Not only do you set up for dominance there, but you also set up for other situations in which you are able to do so much more as well.

Sexy dirty talk boss and worker roleplay

One last roleplay suggestion is that you make use of a situation in which one of you is the boss, and the other is the secretary worker. You can use this as another position of power dirty talk roleplay. Of course, this is another situation where you can naturally find some ways that you will be able to make use of all sorts of dirty talk. You can have the secretary doing every single thing that the boss wants him or her to do. This is a great way that you are able to spice things up—after all, isn't having that control or power great sometimes?

Sexy storytime

Another way that you can really get each other off in the bedroom is to tell a dirty story as you touch the other person. Maybe one of you is jerking off the other as you tell a story to him. You can tell him all about what you want to do or about a fantasy that you have as you are slowly jerking him as foreplay. Make it full of all sorts of dirty talk as you do, and maybe even get into some rough interactions as well if you need to. It's a great way for you to be able to really get into what is going on. Likewise, you can switch off, so he plays with you while he tells you the dirty, sexy story as well. This is a great little switch off in which you are both able to get that fucking that you want, and you are both able to really turn each other on.

Narrate what the other person needs to do with themselves

You can also try adding in the dirty talk by having one of you tell the other person what you want them to do. You can tell your partner to masturbate your way, using all sorts of dirty talk. You could, for example, tell him that you want him to jerk his cock harder in your face with his balls dangling. You could tell her that you want to see her handle those big tits, pinching her nipples. You get a show out of telling and narrating what you want the other person to do. And because you are able to get that show out of it, you can really spice up that bedroom. It may not be typical to have yourself and your partner masturbating for each other, but it can be enjoyable in the moment. You can even do this over sexting as well to really up the ante and make things hotter.

Sexy narrated blow jobs

If your partner has a cock, this one is for you. You want to make sure that you are giving your partner exactly what he or she wants, and you can do that easily through making use of dirty talk that will blow both of your minds. You will be able to figure out exactly what matters the most in your relationship, and you will figure out how best to ensure that everyone is getting along the right way. All you have to do is make sure that you talk dirty as you suck on his cock.

When you are sucking on him, every now and then, you can moan as if you love every moment. Tell him how much you like to suck on it or how much you like to let your teeth run along it. Tell him to talk dirty to you or to grab your hair and guide you while he talks to you about what he wants.

This can go both ways as well. The woman can get licked and do the talking as well.

Blindfold and dirty talk narration

You can try adding in a blindfold to your relationship too, and if you really wanted to enjoy it, you would have the person who is not blindfolded narrating what he or she is about to do to the other person as it happens. As you do this, you encourage the other person to hear you out and build up sexual tension as well. This is a wonderful way that you will be able to enjoy every moment of that dirty talk as you fuck.

Think about it—what could be sexier than having someone else narrate how they are going to fuck you, just before they do it and when you can't see what they are doing? It can be highly erotic. You can even change things up by blindfolding him first and then taking him somewhere else that he doesn't expect.

Let him/her beg for sex as you deny it—for the time being

Another way to really build up that sexual tension is to tease and tease your partner, through dirty talk, through touch, and any other methods that you may choose to make use of. Perhaps you have a game to it—you are only willing to put out if they do something, but you don't tell them what that something is, and they spend the day trying to convince you what it will take. There are so many options for this—perhaps the magic solution is that you want them to say something in particular—perhaps you want them to literally beg for that sex. You would then use dirty talk to lead them to that particular answer. "How bad does that hot little pussy want me?" or "What will you do to get me to fuck you?" As you lead with all sorts of other dirty talk, you will probably find that your partner is willing to do a lot—and as soon as he or she begs, you then give in because that was what you had decided was going to be the cue.

Dirty talk teasing game

Most people know about the typical drinking games where everyone watches these movies together, and at certain points, there are shots taken. It could be that, for example, you take a shot when the main characters say something that is particularly cringe-worthy. However, have you ever played the dirty talk version? For this game, you and your partner will find some porn that the two of you can enjoy. You will then make a list of different actions that are worth different scores, so to speak. If you hear the woman in the video moan or whine, you may say that you are going to make out for thirty seconds, hands off. If you hear dirty talk in the video, you may have to say something yourself toward the other person and get them involved as well. Set up your scoreboard and let it go.

Dirty talk challenge

Another way that you can spice up the bedroom is by trying the dirty talk challenge. This will serve as foreplay all day long. You will effectively be tasked with messaging your partner all day long as much as is reasonable with your own dirty talk. The goal is that you have to keep his mind on you for most of the day. You want to make sure that he can't think about what he is supposed to be doing so that you can take advantage yourself. Make it as creative as you can and try to make sure that you keep him or her turned on as much as possible all day long.

Write a sexy letter

For partners that you are a bit closer to, you can let your creative juices flow, and hopefully, some erotic juices as well. Take some time to write a letter to your partner with all sorts of dirty talk. The idea is to have your partner turned on without touching him or her once—just by creating the letter and handing it off to them. If you can do this, you will be able to make him, or her want you at will. You will spice up your bedroom by adding in an instant turn on, and you will be able to enjoy everything as well.

If you want to add a different twist to this game, you could write erotica yourself, featuring you and your partner, and then act it out, step by step by step. Make sure that it is plenty steamy—make sure that it is a turn on and that it is also something that you can both enjoy.

Find a porn video that you both like… and reenact it

Now, porn is rarely actually good sex. There is sex that looks good, and there is sex that feels good, and the sex that is able to hit both of those points at the same time is exceedingly rare. However, you might get lucky and find it. Choose out some porn and watch it together, enacting everything that you see so that you can enjoy each and every moment of it as well. If you can do this regularly, you will find that you will totally spice up what you are doing, and you will drive your partner crazy.

Read erotica to each other

Find some erotica online and read it with each other. You can take turns reading it out loud with each other, getting used to the dirty words, and potentially even finding some stuff that you would enjoy trying out yourself if you happen to get lucky. Try out the moves that you read about in the erotica and see if it is actually as sexy to act out as it is to read about. Who knows, you might find your next favorite position this way! There are plenty of different websites online where you can find all sorts of great erotica, free of charge and without any strings attached, meaning you don't have to leave home or buy anything at all to do this.

Mix and match

You can also put several of these different challenges together to really up the ante on it all. If you want to have mind-blowing sex, you need to be willing to experiment and to make sure that ultimately, you enjoy what you are doing. It may be unconventional, but there is nothing wrong with that. It may involve copious amounts of dirty talk, but there is nothing wrong with that, either. It may involve all sorts of things or positions that you never thought you would do, but that's okay too. Sex is one of those things that is not, by any means, one size fits all. There are so many different options out there for you that you can do, and there are many things that some people swear by that would make other people blanch. So long as you and your partner are finding that it is hot, that is all that matters!

Conclusion

And with that, we have made it to the end of this book. Hopefully, you have read this book with your partner and took the time to really get to know what it is that you and your partner really want. It is important that if you are going to be intimate with someone, whether they are a one night stand, a long-term partner, or even your spouse, you want to make sure that you are communicating.

Dirty talk itself is just another form of communication, but it is one that must be preceded by other concepts as well. If you want to use dirty talk to turn your partner on, you want to make sure that you are always engaging in the right kinds of behaviors. You want to make sure that ultimately, you and your partner are on the right page with everything, and if you can be on the same page as each other, you can usually ensure that the sex that you will have will be mind-blowing. After all, nothing is better than fucking someone that is naturally going to follow your moves, pay attention to your particular desires, and make sure that you are happy. If you can do this, you will have plenty of success.

Before you dive right into dirty talking with your partner, then make sure that you communicate. Is it sexy to talk about boundaries? Not traditionally, but you are conveying your own emotions and that you care about the other person and their boundaries, which is highly erotic itself. Make sure that you and your partner are on the same page with everything that you do so that you will be able to control your enjoyment as well.

From there, all you have to do is get creative. When you know what each other's boundaries are, you can get to work, physically and mentally as well. You can send dirty messages to your partner. You can beg them to fuck you or to let you fuck them. You can encourage them to do things that you may normally have been too afraid to say. You can make sure that you are in complete and utter control over your sexual relationship, and if you can make that happen, you are going to find that your sex life will be better than ever. You can teach your partner to crave you more than anything else. You can teach your partner to want you constantly, or that you can turn him or her on in an instant just by knowing what they like to hear and how you can really tickle that fancy and get them going. All you need to do is make sure that when you are talking to your partner, you are spending the time to be erotic.

Remember, all you need to do is describe what is happening. Remember that there are three keys here: Say what you are going to do, what you are doing, and what you just did. If you can be descriptive like this, you don't even have to think much about the dirty talk that is happening. All you have to do is just that—narrate what you are doing so that your partner will be even more turned on. Maybe you tell him, "I'm going to ride your hard cock." Then, you say, "Ooh, I love riding your hard cock." Later, when you are done, you can say, "I'm so glad I got to ride your cock." You are essentially just regurgitating out one sentiment in three different ways, but this descriptiveness is a great way to not only turn your partner on because you know that you are already saying things that are narrating actions that happen to turn your partner on.

You should also remember that expressing your desire is crucial as well, especially if you do it with commands. These are all keys to making sure that you can drive your partner wild, and if you can remember these point sand take them into your bedroom with you, you will find that you are highly successful with everything that you are doing. All you need to do is make sure that you are effective in what you are doing.

Thank you for taking the time to read through this book, and remember, dirty talk is a skill. Just like any other skill, it can be natural for some people, but for most, it is something that will take effort and practice. You must commit to what you are doing. You must make sure that you are taking the time to practice and that you are willing to deal with the trial and error. It may not always be the most fun, and it may be embarrassing sometimes, but if you can remember to keep on going, you can learn to say all sorts of things that will turn your partner on instantly so that you can have the time, or the fuck, of your life.

Finally, if you found that this book was beneficial in providing you with tips that will help you to properly master foreplay through dirty talk, or if you feel like the information and activities will help to spice up your sex life, please consider heading over and leaving a review with your experience. It could help others find the information that they need to get it going on in bed too, and it would also be greatly appreciated! Your feedback is always well received and helps to ensure that future books are even better than the last ones. Thank you, once more, and good luck, with all your bedroom adventures! May your fucking be fun, and may your orgasms be mind-blowing!

Thank You

You could have picked from dozens of other books, but you picked our bundle of 2 books

How to Talk Dirty:
Transform Your Sex Life & Spike Up Your Libido. 200 Real Dirty Talk Tips to Drive Your Partner Wild. Make Your Partner Your "Sex Slave"

So, THANK YOU for getting this book and for making it all the way to the end.

Could you please consider posting a review on Amazon or if you get the Audio version then on Audible?

Posting a positive review is the best and easiest way to support the work of independent authors like me.

Your feedback will help me to keep writing the kind of books that will help you get the results you want.

It can be something short and simple ☺

Thank you so much

>> Leave a review on Amazon US <<

>> Leave a review on Amazon UK <<

www.ingramcontent.com/pod-product-compliance
Lightning Source LLC
Chambersburg PA
CBHW072002290426
44109CB00018B/2107